# Australia's Incredible Insects

JESSA THURMAN

Australian Geographic
Hardie Grant
CHILDREN'S PUBLISHING

Photograph: Shutterstock.

# Australia's Incredible Insects

Australian Geographic

# CONTENTS

## FACT

While beetles are the most diverse group of insects, weevils are the most diverse group of beetles.

# INTRODUCTION

## WHAT IS AN INSECT?

**Insects are animals (Kingdom Animalia) as they have multiple cells, feed on other organisms, can move, respond to their environment quickly, and typically reproduce with a mate. Insects are also part of a unique group of animals with a hard exoskeleton, called arthropods (Phylum Arthropoda). Arthropods are unique in that they lack a backbone and must shed their exoskeleton or moult in order to grow.**

**THIS SMALL BOTTLE CICADA** *(Glaucopsaltria viridis)* is moulting into an adult. First it slowly emerges from a split in its back, removing its entire body. The cicada then inflates its wings and lets them dry before it can fly. You may have seen the exoskeleton left over from the moulting process, it can look just like an insect, but there's nothing inside.

Unlike other arthropods including spiders, scorpions, and millipedes, insects only have six legs, two antennae, three main body segments (head, thorax, and abdomen), and usually two pairs of wings. Here you can see the **32-SPOTTED KATYDID** *(Ephippitytha trigintiduoguttata)* with each of these body parts. It also has a set of specialised mouthparts for eating gum leaves and two compound eyes made of thousands of ommatidia that detect colour and brightness. It also has six legs, but the hind legs are adapted for jumping.

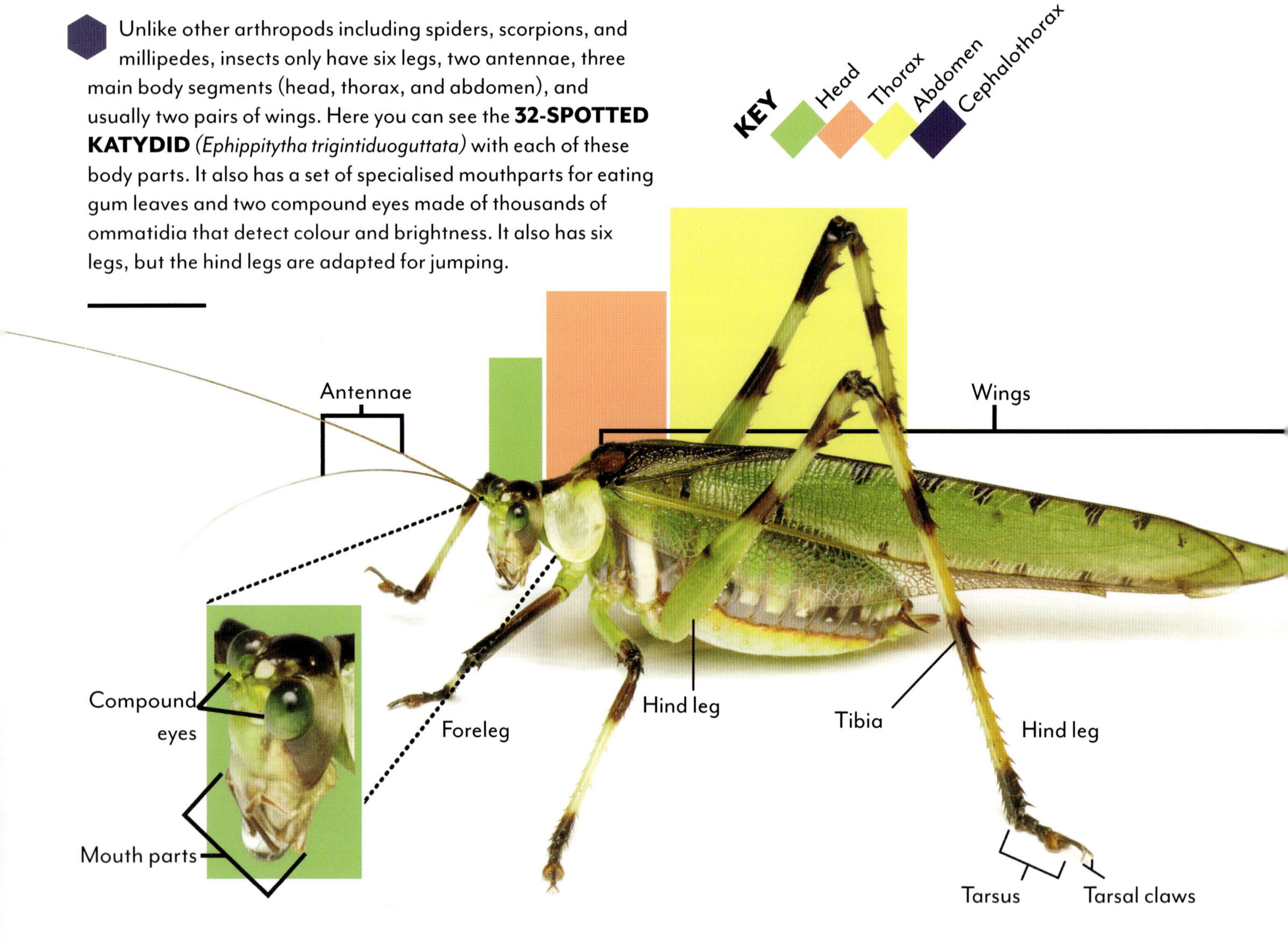

KEY
Head
Thorax
Abdomen
Cephalothorax

Antennae
Wings
Compound eyes
Mouth parts
Foreleg
Hind leg
Tibia
Hind leg
Tarsus
Tarsal claws

**SPIDERS ARE NOT INSECTS.** Instead, they belong to a group called arachnids (Class Arachnida) which have two body segments: an abdomen and a cephalothorax. They also have four pairs of legs, no antennae, and no wings.

**THE TEDDY BEAR BEE** *(Amegilla bombiformis)* also has the three main body sections and two pairs of wings. The front pair of wings is called the forewings while the back is called the hindwings. Female bees have stingers or ovipositors which are a modified egg-laying organ.

**Photograph:** Alan Henderson – Minibeast Wildlife.

**FACT**

**Insects do not have lungs! Instead, they breathe through a series of tubes called tracheae.**

Beetles like the **RAINBOW LEAF BEETLE** *(Spilopyra sumptuosa)* have their forewings hardened into two coverings called elytra. Underneath the elytra are the hindwings which can fold out when the beetle needs to fly.

# ORGANISING LIFE

**The study of insects is called entomology. The scientists who study insects are entomologists and their research can include describing species (taxonomy), conserving insects and their habitats, exploring novel chemicals for medical research, and controlling pests in agriculture and for disease control.**

**Photograph:** Hongming Kan.

**INSECTS ARE THE LARGEST GROUP OF ANIMALS,** representing roughly 70% of all animal species on Earth. Of this global diversity, approximately 35% are beetles (Order Coleoptera) with over 350,000 species known. The other most diverse groups are wasps, bees, and ants (Order Hymenoptera) and flies (Order Diptera) with approximately 150,000 species described from each group so far.

**ROUGHLY ONE MILLION SPECIES OF INSECTS** from around the world have been described so far. However, it is estimated that we have roughly 4.5 million insect species left to be named! In Australia, over 62,000 insect species have been described, but we anticipate over 130,000 species are left to be named. Describing a species is only the start to understanding one, so with approximatelt 31% of insects in Australia described, there is much more to be known!

**IN THIS BOOK,** you'll learn about the different groups of insects based on their taxonomy. Each chapter will showcase at least one new order of insects, like beetles (Order Coleoptera). Each chapter is then further divided into different Families, like stag beetles.

**KINGDOM**
Animalia
(Animals)

**PHYLUM**
Arthropoda
(Arthropods)

**CLASS**
Insecta
(Insects)

**ORDER**
Coleoptera
(Beetles)

**FAMILY**
Lucanidae
(Stag beetles)

**GENUS**
*Phalacrognathus*

**SPECIES**
*P.muelleri*
(Rainbow stag beetle)

## NAMES

**While they can be difficult to remember, scientific names are vital to studying insects. Aside from the relationships that they reflect, scientific names are universal. Common names can change from place to place or person to person. Scientific names are meant to unite across languages and cultures.**

**HERE YOU CAN SEE THE RAINBOW STAG BEETLE**

*Phalacrognathus muelleri* is an animal, an arthropod, an insect, a beetle, and a stag beetle, by exploring its classification or taxonomy. This classification helps us understand how these animals may have evolved over time by showing what they are most closely related to. These relationships have historically been based on appearance or morphology of an insect, but more recently this has been combined with DNA studies.

**To learn more about stag beetles (Family Lucanidae) see page 18.**

# HOW INSECTS GROW

Insect diversity can be overwhelming at first, but it breaks into many different groups called Orders, which the chapters of this book are based around. Before they break into Orders, insects can also be easily divided into two main groups based on how they grow.

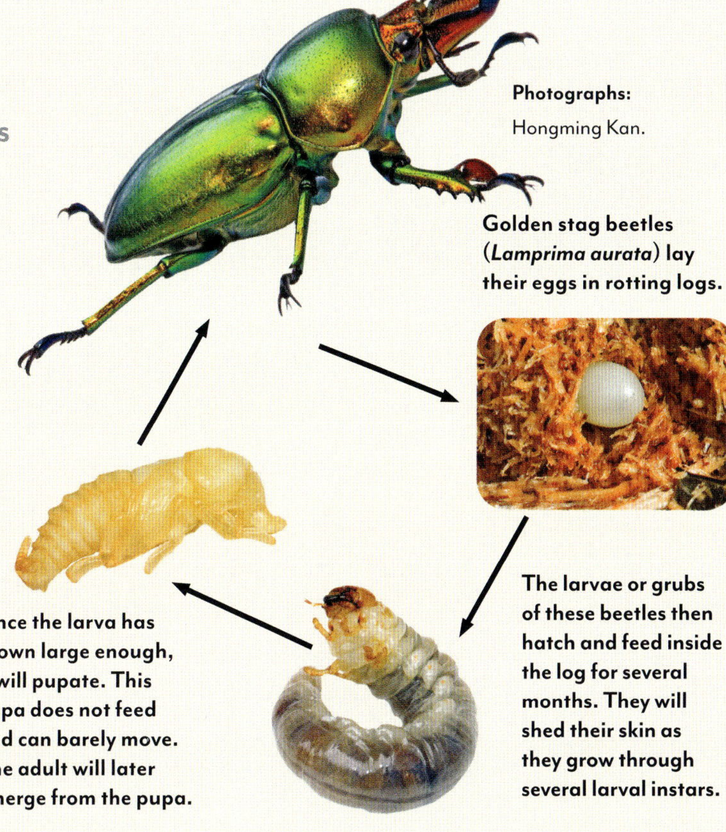

**Photographs:** Hongming Kan.

**Golden stag beetles (*Lamprima aurata*) lay their eggs in rotting logs.**

**The larvae or grubs of these beetles then hatch and feed inside the log for several months. They will shed their skin as they grow through several larval instars.**

**Once the larva has grown large enough, it will pupate. This pupa does not feed and can barely move. The adult will later emerge from the pupa.**

## COMPLETE METAMORPHOSIS

### HOLOMETABOLOUS INSECTS

Insects that have a full life cycle undergo complete metamorphosis, starting as an **EGG**, hatching into a **LARVA**, growing into a **PUPA**, and then emerging as an **ADULT**. In butterflies their larvae are called caterpillars, while beetles are called grubs and flies are called maggots.

## INCOMPLETE METAMORPHOSIS

### HEMIMETABOLOUS INSECTS

The second group of insects undergoes incomplete metamorphosis where they start as an **EGG**, but hatch into a **NYMPH** which slowly grows into an **ADULT**. Nymphs resemble their adult form, but they lack wings. Nymphs also have several stages called instars before they become an adult, gradually growing larger between each moult. Stick insects, grasshoppers and dragonflies all undergo incomplete metamorphosis.

**Dancing leaf insects (*Walaphyllium monteithi*) hatch from seed-like eggs as a black, ant-like nymph. These nymphs soon turn green and search for leaves to feed on.**

**As they go through several nymphal instars, these nymphs look more and more like leaves. Eventually they grow wing buds.**

**By their sixth life stage, male leaf insects will have fully developed wings and be an adult. Females have an extra moult and take longer to reach adulthood. Although their wings develop, females cannot fly.**

CHAPTER 1

# BEETLES

## ORDER COLEOPTERA

The lives of many beetles like this regal jewel beetle have yet to be studied in detail! **Photograph:** Hongming Kan.

# INTRODUCTION

While insects are the most diverse group of animals on the planet, beetles are the most diverse group of insects described.

So far, over 350,000 species of beetles have been described from the world, but many more remain unknown to science. Beetles have a complete life cycle, starting from an egg, hatching to a larva and feeding until it grows large enough to pupate, and then emerge later as an adult.

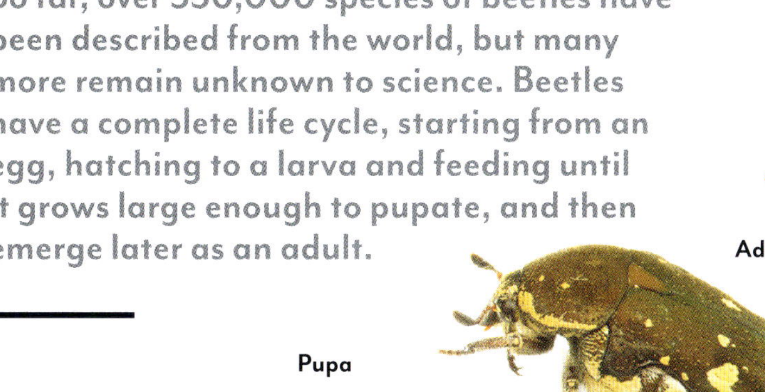


Larvae of the brown flower beetle feed on decaying matter in the soil.

The forewings of beetles have been modified into hardened elytra. These elytra cover and protect the soft hindwings. When a beetle needs to fly, it lifts up the elytra and lets the hindwings unfold and flap.

Beetle larvae are called grubs. Many grubs, like that of this rhino beetle (*Xylotrupes* sp.) are used as food or bait by Indigenous Australians. ^

**Long-nosed lycid beetle.** *(Porrostoma rhipidium)*

# JEWEL BEETLES

## FAMILY BUPRESTIDAE

**Jewel beetles are often considered the gems of the beetle world based on their brilliant metallic colours. Australia has a large diversity of this beautiful group, and you can find them feeding on the flowers of tea tree shrubs (*Leptospermum* spp.) and eucalypt trees. They can be difficult to catch, as they are quick to fly away. They use their flight to escape predators, which a curious entomologist may resemble.**

### WATERHOUSE'S JEWEL BEETLE <

*Pseudotaenia waterhousei*

Adult beetles of this species have been observed emerging from the trunks of wattles (*Acacia doratoxylon* and *A. leiocalyx*), which are common in the dry habitats of central Australia. The adults have not been seen feeding though, making scientists wonder if they feed at all in this stage!

> ***Location:*** *Central regions of New South Wales and Queensland.*

**Photograph:** Hongming Kan.

### REGAL JEWEL BEETLE

*Calodema regalis* ^

This large beetle is rarely seen or collected since it feeds on the flowers of tall trees like White Euodia (*Melicope micrococca)* and Red Bloodwood (*Corymbia gummifera*). Due to its rarity, little is known about this beetle including where it lays its eggs, where and what its larvae feed on, and how long its life cycle takes. Perhaps you may solve the mystery around this species' life history.

> ***Location:*** *Tropical north Queensland to northern New South Wales.*

### SIX-SPOTTED JEWEL BEETLE

*Castiarina sexplagiata* ⌄

This smaller jewel beetle is often found feeding on tea tree flowers (*Leptospermum* spp.), dipping their head into the cup-like flowers to drink the nectar inside. This species can vary in colour, with yellow to orange spots and different patterns. They often fly away when disturbed but can be observed with a patient eye.

> ***Location:*** *East coast of Australia.*

A male jewel beetle attempts to mate with a glass bottle.

Photograph: Dave Rentz.

## ORANGE JEWEL BEETLE

*Julodimorpha bakewelli* < >

Orange jewel beetle larvae live in the roots of gum trees (*Eucalyptus* spp.) where they feed on the developing tissue of the tree. Adult beetles feed on flowers, like those on wattle shrubs and can be found around dawn or dusk.

< **Location:** *Arid and semi-arid regions of Queensland, New South Wales, Victoria, South Australia and Western Australia.*

AUSTRALIA

## BEETLES LOVE BOTTLES?

In the 1980s, Western Australia's discarded stubby bottles were a 'love trap' for these orange jewel beetles. Male beetles were attracted to the shiny, orange, and bumpy bottles, which looked like the ultimate female. They would try to mate with the bottle until they died. Researchers discovered this fatal attraction and modified the bottle to be less attractive to the beetle. This saved countless beetles.

## YELLOW SPOTTED JEWEL BEETLE

*Austrophorella quadrisignata* <

This species is the only one in the genus *Austrophorella* and it is unique to Australia. It can be found in dry areas of central Queensland and the larvae feed inside the stems of the soap tree (*Alphitonia excelsa*).

> **Location:** *Central regions of Queensland.*

AUSTRALIA

## VARIABLE JEWEL BEETLE

*Temognatha variabilis* >

The variable jewel beetle can range in colours, being bright yellow, dark red, or anything in between. Aside from feeding on flowers, adults of this species can be found on she-oak (*Allocasuarina* spp.) trunks or branches where they lay their eggs. While this species has not been observed collecting materials, it has specialised structures on its egg-laying organ (ovipositor) and is thought to collect sand or charcoal from burned trees to later use for covering their eggs.

> **Location:** *Coastal regions of New South Wales, Queensland, South Australia and Victoria.*

Photograph: Hongming Kan.

## STRIPED JEWEL BEETLE

*Temognatha alternata* ^

Despite being large and lovely, this jewel beetle has no formal species description! In 1889, Carl Lumholtz published a name for this species without a description. He likely found it while camping with Indigenous Australians.

> **Location:** *Tropical North Queensland.*

# GROUND BEETLES FAMILY CARABIDAE

**Ground beetles are important predators that can be found in hot deserts, riverbanks, and even cold mountain tops. While some of these beetles have lost their ability to fly, many are well-adapted for running and chasing their prey.**

## GIANT RAINFOREST GROUND BEETLE

*Nurus* sp. ^

While they are voracious predators at night, the giant rainforest ground beetle hides away in its burrow during the day, much like a bear in a cave. These beetles construct their own unique burrows under tree roots, rocks, and logs and keep the entrance to their burrow, clear of any leaves. Only one beetle lives within each burrow, but in the wet season, males will emerge from their burrows to search for females.

> ***Location:*** *Rainforests of Queensland and New South Wales.*

**Female giant rainforest ground beetles** enclose their yellow eggs in a mud-case. The beetle will then guard over her eggs in her burrow. ^

## GREEN-LINED GROUND BEETLE

*Catadromus* sp. >

These large beetles can be seen along riverbeds, quickly running across the ground and catching prey. Some species even eat frogs! One species (*C. lacordairei*) is listed as vulnerable to extinction in Tasmania. This is likely due to habitat loss as their swamps and riverbanks are under threat from development and pollution.

^ ***Location:*** *Riverbeds throughout Australia.*

## RAINFOREST TIGER BEETLE

*Distipsidera* sp. <

Tiger beetles are incredibly fast runners that have enormous jaws and eyes. These traits make them successful predators and species can be found hunting along riverbanks or tree trunks, like this rainforest tiger beetle. Their larvae are predators too. They use their flat head to plug their burrow entrance, and when prey walks across it, they pop up to grab it! If you're fast enough to catch a tiger beetle, watch out for their bite!

> ***Location:*** *Rainforests of Queensland and New South Wales.*

### FACT

**The fastest insect on the planet is a species of South Australian tiger beetle (*Cicindela hudsoni*). It can run up to 2.5m per second or up to 9km per hour!**

# LONGHORN BEETLES

## FAMILY CERAMBYCIDAE

**Longhorn beetles or longicorns are named after their exceptionally long antennae which are often several times longer than their body! Adult beetles have strong mandibles for chewing through wood. Their larvae often develop in stressed trees, while some feed in dead or decaying wood.**

Photograph: Hongming Kan.

### POINCIANA LONGICORN

*Agrianome spinicollis* <

These enormous beetles begin their lives in dead tree limbs. The larvae feed on decaying wood and can tunnel into the living tree to feed on growth tissue there. After several months, they pupate inside the wood, and emerge near summer to reproduce.

> ***Location:*** *East coast of Australia.*

### RAINFOREST LONGHORN

*Rosenbergia megalocephala* <

This is one of the largest longhorn beetles found in Australia. Their large mandibles or jaws can easily chew through bark or the tender skin of a young entomologist's hands! They feed on sap flows and lay their eggs in the bark of decaying trees.

> ***Location:*** *Tropical North Queensland Australia.*

### WASP MIMICKING LONGHORN BEETLE

*Hesthesis* sp. ^

This longhorn beetle mimics a large wasp. Its elytra are short, while its hindwings are always visible and will be held out like a wasps' wings, while its body has yellow and black stripes. But appearance isn't enough, this beetle also acts like a wasp by buzzing its wings and raising its abdomen as though it can sting.

∨ ***Location:*** *Throughout coastal regions of Australia.*

### PLUM LONGHORN BEETLE

*Acalolepta* sp.

Eggs of this beetle are laid on the bark of Burdekin plum trees (*Pleiogynium timoriense*). When their larvae hatch out, they bore into the trunk where they feed for several months. Once it is large enough, the larva crawls just under the bark and chews a large circle. The bark inside this circle eventually dries and falls away, exposing a hole in the centre that goes further into the tree. This mark on the tree looks like a bullseye. The larva pupates in the tunnel and will later emerge as an adult beetle. If too many beetles are in one tree, they can kill the tree!

> ***Location:*** *East coast of Australia and the Northern Territory.*

# LEAF BEETLES

## FAMILY CHRYSOMELIDAE

**Leaf beetles feed on leaves both as adults and as larvae. Australia has a large diversity of eucalypt-feeding leaf beetles and some of the larvae use eucalyptus oil as a defence.**

### ORANGE SPOTTED LEAF BEETLE

*Paropsisterna sexpustulata* >

These beetles feed on the leaves of eucalypts and many other plants. When they aren't feeding, these beetles will hide under bark. The black and orange colouration may serve as a sign to predators that this beetle tastes bad, however these beetles tend to be more active at night when fewer things may see them.

> ***Location:*** *Open forests of Queensland, New South Wales and Victoria.*

These colourful beetles live in dark rainforests.

### RAINBOW LEAF BEETLE

*Spilopyra sumptuosa* ^

These rainbow leaf beetles can be surprisingly hard to spot. Their vibrant colours are the result of a structural colouration where the colour is produced by unique reflections on the surface of the beetle's body. Despite its beauty, this colouration is considered a type of camouflage. As light reflects off the beetle, it can distort the shape, making it difficult for predators to see the beetle.

> ***Location:*** *Southeast Queensland and northern New South Wales.*

# LADY BEETLES/LADYBIRDS

## FAMILY COCCINELLIDAE

**Ladybirds are a diverse group of beetles and many species are predators both as adults and larvae. Some species will lay their eggs in colonies of aphids or scale insects to ensure their larvae will have plenty of food.**

### TRANSVERSE LADYBIRD

*Coccinella transversalis* ∟

The transverse ladybird is a generalist predator, meaning it can feed on a wide variety of prey. These prey include many pests like aphids, mites, scale insects, and caterpillars. Farmers use beetles like these for biological control, a sustainable pest management strategy. Instead of using harmful insecticides, natural enemies like these beetles can be used to control pests.

> ***Location:*** *Throughout Australia and southeast Asia.*

Photograph: Ben Revell.

### STRIPED LADYBIRD

*Micraspis frenata* ^

Some ladybirds will hibernate over winter! You can find large numbers of them gathered under logs, rocks, and sometimes inside your pantry. This helps them stay safe and warm.

> ***Location:*** *Throughout the east coast of Australia and Tasmania.*

# WEEVILS FAMILY CURCULIONIDAE

**The most diverse group of beetles! Weevils look like little elephants of the insect world, with their long rostrum or nose which has their mouthparts and antennae at the end.**

## ELEPHANT WEEVIL

*Orthorhinus cylindrirostris* ^

Elephant weevils are common in the coastal regions of Australia where they feed on plant tissue like the stems of wattles. They get their name from their long snout and can be identified by their forelegs which are larger and longer than their other legs.

> ***Location:*** *East coast of Australia.*

## BOTANY BAY DIAMOND WEEVIL

*Chrysolopus spectabilis* ^

The Botany Bay diamond weevil was one of the first insects collected and described from Australia. This first specimen was collected by Joseph Banks on his voyage with Captain Cook. Today, adults can still be found commonly feeding on wattles (*Acacia* spp.), while their larvae feed on the roots.

# CLICK BEETLES FAMILY ELATERIDAE

**Click beetles have a special adaptation for escaping predators: they can snap their thorax with enough force that it launches them away from any threat. This movement also produces a 'click' sound.**

**Photograph:** César Puechmarin.

**Fireflies make night-time magical.**

# FIREFLIES FAMILY LAMPYRIDAE

## FLASHING FIREFLIES

*Atyphella* spp. >

Australian fireflies can be seen flashing either singly or in synchrony shortly after dusk in mangroves and rainforests. Male fireflies will fly and flash light from the luminous organs at the end of their abdomen. These flashes are signalling females in the leaf litter which may flash back to the males flying above. Males have large eyes to help them see females flashing. Once a male finds a female that is signalling, he will fly down to her to mate. Adult fireflies are not known to eat and only spend a few days in this stage.

> ***Location:*** *East coast of Australia.*

# STAG BEETLES

FAMILY LUCANIDAE

**Stag beetles can be easily identified as the males of this group have large mandibles or jaws. These beetles are named after these large mandibles which resemble the horns of a stag deer. Males use this unique trait to fight with each other to access females or food that females need. Females lack these large mandibles and have sometimes been mistaken for a different species!**

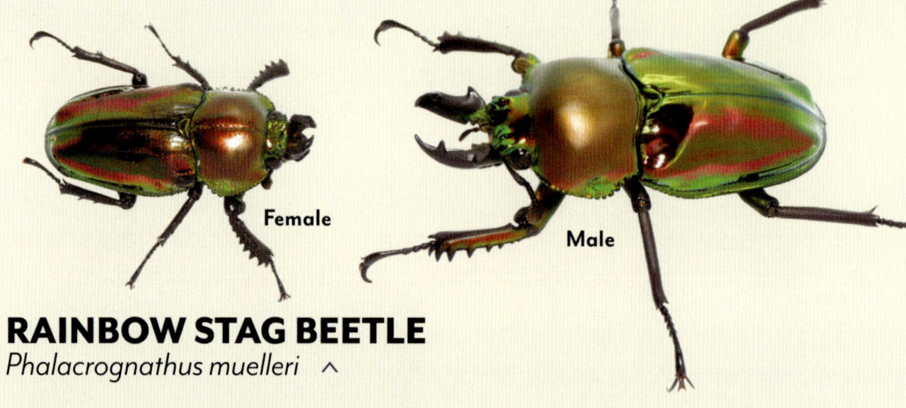


## RAINBOW STAG BEETLE

*Phalacrognathus muelleri* ^

Rainbow stag beetles spend much of their life in the dark. Their larvae feed in rotting logs, taking nine months to grow large enough to pupate. Once the adults emerge from their pupal case, they begin their search for rotting fruit or sap flows. Females have a simple task to find food, but males must find food and a female, often fighting with other males for access to each.

> ***Location:*** *Tropical North Queensland.*

**Photograph:** Hongming Kan.

**Photograph:** Hongming Kan.

## GOLDEN STAG BEETLE

*Lamprima aurata* <

The golden stag beetle is not always golden. In fact, this species can be purple, blue, green, red, or golden yellow! This variation in colour is likely why so many different species of *Lamprima* were described from Australia. These different coloured beetles have since been found to all belong to the same species, but there are unique species found on Lord Howe Island and Norfolk Island.

> ***Location:*** *Coastal regions of Queensland, New South Wales, Victoria, South Australia, Tasmania and Western* Australia.

**Golden stag beetles** also feed in rotting logs, but are more widespread than the large, rainbow stag beetles. These smaller beetles also have males with large jaws that fight with each other for access to females and sap flows. Their variation in colour is thought to be linked to their genetics.

## BROWN STAG BEETLE

*Ryssonotus nebulosus* >

Brown stag beetles spend nearly all their lives in rotting logs, with adults rarely seen outside of them! When these beetles are wet, their brown colours appear black. However, once they dry, the unique brown and black patterns can be seen.

> ***Location:*** *Coastal areas of Queensland and New South Wales.*

# NET-WINGED BEETLES

### LONG-NOSED LYCID BEETLE

*Porrostoma rhipidium* >

These beetles feed on nectar and can often be found on flowering plants. Their bright colours help to advertise that these beetles are toxic to predators. In fact, many insects have converged on this colouration pattern to share the same message: "don't eat me, I will make you sick."

^ ***Location:*** *East coast of Australia, South Australia, Tasmania and Victoria.*

# BESS OR FAMILY BEETLES

## FAMILY PASSALIDAE

**Bess beetles spend their lives making quiet noises. As adults, they can make wheezy sounds by rubbing their abdomen and elytra together. They likely do this to alert others to predators or to frighten a predator away from their hissing noise.**

### BLACK BESS BEETLE

*Aulacocyclus kaupii* ^

> ***Location:*** *Coastal habitats of Queensland.*

**As larvae, they make noises using a stubby set of hindlegs and a stridulatory file. When you first see a larva, you may think it only has two pairs of legs, but closer inspection reveals this oddly adapted third pair of legs. They use this last pair to make noises!**

**Since both adults and larvae can make sounds and they are often found together, it is thought that these squeaks are also them communicating with each other.**

### LARGE BESS BEETLE

*Mastachilus quaestionis* ∨

This large bess beetle is around 5cm long and spends much of its life in dark cavities of rotting logs. Once it is done feeding or breeding in one log, it will move to a new one, sometimes flying long distances. But when it leaves, it does not leave alone. Aside from their family groups, bess beetles often have little mites that live on them. In this case, large male and female mites (*Megisthanus* sp.) can be seen living on this beetle. These mites cause no harm to the beetle and instead feed on fungi and other small arthropods which can be found in the tunnels that the beetles live in. By tagging along on the bess beetle, these mites are able to be carried around from log to log, like a free shuttle service.

> ***Location:*** *Rainforests of southeast Queensland.*

# DARKLING BEETLES

## FAMILY TENEBRIONIDAE

### PIE DISH BEETLE

*Pterohelaeus* sp. >

These beetles get their name from the flanges extending off their body which resemble the edges of a pie dish. They are common throughout Australia and forage at night. Desert species bury themselves in sand during the day, while others hide under bark.

> **Location:** *Throughout coastal and desert regions of Australia.*

### BUMPY FUNGUS BEETLE

*Byrsax macleayi* ¬

Once the sun sets, these fungus beetles will crawl out from their hiding places and feed on large bracket fungi which grow on dying trees. Male beetles have two large horns on their head. They likely use these to fight with other males for females or for access to fungi. These beetles also have a terrible defensive smell.

> **Location:** *Rainforests of southeast Queensland and New South Wales.*

# SCARAB BEETLES

## FAMILY SCARABAEIDAE

## FLOWER CHAFERS

### SUBFAMILY CETONIINAE

**Flower chafers are a diverse group of beetles, each with a unique pattern and life history.**

### BROWN FLOWER BEETLE

*Glycyphana stolata* >

These small, brown beetles are a common sight in summer. You can find them feeding on flowers, especially bottlebrush. They spend the rest of the year as larvae in the soil of gardens. They pupate here and form an egg-like shell made of dirt.

> **Location:** *Coastal regions throughout Australia.*

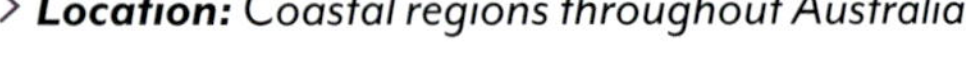

### FIDDLER BEETLE

*Eupoecila australasiae* <

These beetles are common in heathland and parks. Their larvae feed in rotting logs and can also be found with the larvae of stag beetles.

< **Location:** *Coastal regions of Queensland, New South Wales, Victoria and South Australia.*

## RHINO BEETLES

### SUBFAMILY DYNASTINAE

### AUSTRALIAN RHINO BEETLE

*Xylotrupes australicus* ^

Male rhino beetles have two horns, one on their head and one on their thorax. They use these to fight with other males for access to sap flows and the females that are attracted to these sites. Like all beetles, their forewings are hardened into protective elytra which shield their delicate hindwings. The beetles fly by lifting their elytra to unfurl their hindwings. When disturbed, they also make a hissing noise by rubbing their abdomen against their elytra. Their larvae are large C-shaped grubs that can often be found in compost heaps.

> **Location:** *East coast of Queensland and New South Wales.*

# CHRISTMAS BEETLES

## SUBFAMILY RUTELINAE

Christmas beetles can be found across Australia. This common name refers to many species within the genus *Anoplognathus*, so be careful to find out which one you are talking about! Christmas beetles feed on eucalypt leaves as adults, and roots as larvae. The adults emerge around December, and are attracted to lights.

### CHRISTMAS BEETLE

*Anoplognathus porosus* ^

> **Location:** *East coast of Queensland, New South Wales and Victoria.*

### Save the koala and save the Christmas Beetle

In the past, hundreds of these beetles could be found in summer, but very few are seen today. This is likely due to clearing eucalypt forests that these beetles depend on. By saving these habitats, we can protect species like the Christmas beetles and koalas from extinction.

### GREEN CHRISTMAS BEETLE

*Anoplognathus punctulatus* ^

> **Location:** *Tropical North Queensland.*

# DUNG BEETLES

## SUBFAMILY SCARABAEINAE

Most dung beetles feed on the poop made by other animals, and in this way are key nutrient recyclers in nature. Some dung beetles will build burrows underneath piles of dung, while others will roll balls of it away.

### HOMEMADE DUNG BEETLE

*Cephalodesmius* sp. ^

While most dung beetles collect poop, these curious ones are a little more 'cultured.' They collect plant material, culturing their own homemade dung. They prepare underground burrows where they take leaves and flowers, and once they've made enough of their fake dung, the female makes balls of it with an egg in each. That egg hatches into a beetle larva, which feeds inside the ball, growing and hollowing it out while mum adds more to the outside.

> **Location:** *East coast of Queensland and New South Wales.*

**Photograph:** Dr. Andrew Maynard.

### GIANT DUNG BEETLE

*Aulacopris maximus* ^

The giant dung beetle is the largest of its kind in Australia, but it likes some of the smallest poo: bat guano. They can be found in caves with bats or in hollow trees found in rainforests. Some bats will roost in these trees and the giant dung beetle will collect the bat poo to form balls for its young.

> **Location:** *Rainforests of southeast Queensland and northern New South Wales.*

### COMMON DUNG BEETLE

*Onthophagus neostenocerus* ^

These small dung beetles can be found sitting on leaves at night, roughly half a meter off the ground. They use this perch to smell out any fresh dung being laid. When a waft of the good stuff comes their way, they follow the scent to the new pile of dung.

> **Location:** *East coast of Australia.*

# CHAPTER 2

# BEES AND WASPS

## ORDER HYMENOPTERA

Did you know that not all bees sting?

# INTRODUCTION

Bees and wasps are only one half of the order Hymenoptera, a group also composed of ants and sawflies which are included in the next chapter. Bees and wasps are most known for their painful sting, but this behaviour has originally developed as a defence or way to paralyse prey. Many wasps can sting, but not all of them do! While some bees and wasps are social, living in hives of many individuals, most species are solitary, living on their own.

**WASPS**

## FACT

Only female bees, wasps, and ants can sting! A stinger is a modified egg-laying organ called an ovipositor. The fluid is originally used to help lay an egg, but has evolved in some to paralyse prey.

**BEES**

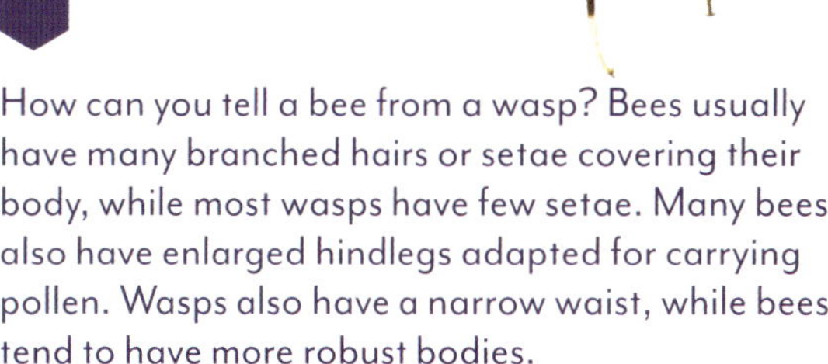

How can you tell a bee from a wasp? Bees usually have many branched hairs or setae covering their body, while most wasps have few setae. Many bees also have enlarged hindlegs adapted for carrying pollen. Wasps also have a narrow waist, while bees tend to have more robust bodies.

## IMPORTANT POLLINATORS!

Both bees and wasps are important pollinators. Even though most wasps hunt prey or parasitise a host, they also need to feed on nectar. Different body sizes in bees and wasps can also make them more efficient pollinators.

## LIFE CYCLE OF BEES AND WASPS

Most bees that you see are female! The workers of the hive are all female bees.

# BEES

## CLADE ANTHOPHILA

# SOCIAL BEES

## FAMILY APIDAE

Social bees live in a hive with a queen, who lays all the eggs. These bees work together like cells of a body, as they are all closely related. Worker bees are all daughters of the queen, and they gather pollen and nectar, defend the hive, and care for the larvae of the queen. Male bees, also called drones, are rare and only appear when there are new queens to mate with. Few species of bees are social, but there are some unique social species found here in Australia including some that can be kept in hives.

### A HONEYBEE CAN STING ONLY ONCE!

Honeybees have a barbed stinger or ovipositor. When they sting something, they cannot pull their stinger back out and instead damage their abdomen, digestive tract and muscles in this process. Sadly as a result, they die.

### EUROPEAN HONEYBEE

*Apis mellifera* ^

European Honeybees are used to pollinate our crops on a large scale and produce most of the honey that you can buy. Some honey advertises the specific flowers that the bees have foraged on and can have unique flavours from this. These bees, while in Australia, are not native and in some cases they are thought to be harmful, competing with our native bee species for access to nectar resources.

> ***Location:*** *Throughout Australia.*

### NATIVE STINGLESS BEE

*Tetragonula carbonaria* and *T. hockingsi* v

Several species of bees are called the 'stingless bee' in Australia, but there are two species which are more commonly kept in hives or found nesting in trees. These two species can be hard to tell apart, but one (*Tetragonula carbonaria*) makes a circular or spiral set of brood cells, which house the bee larvae. The other species (*T. hockingsi*) has an irregular arrangement of brood cells. Each species collects pollen and makes honey by consuming flower nectar. These are stored in pollen and honeypots in the hive and used to feed to their brood, or bee larvae. These brood are cared for by their sisters, the worker bees until they develop into adults.

> ***Location:*** *Northern regions of Western Australia and the Northern Territory, and along the east coast of Australia.*

Stingless bees are an important food and medicine resource to Indigenous Australians.

# GIANT DIGGER BEES
## TRIBE ANTHOPHORINI

### BLUE-BANDED BEE
*Amegilla spp.* ^

Blue-banded bees are named after the striking blue stripes on their abdomen, but a few species look very similar. These bees are all known as buzz-pollinators. When they visit a flower, you may hear the buzz from them using their flight muscles to vibrate the flower. This dislodges pollen and allows them to pollinate several flowers that other pollinators cannot. Blue-banded bees can be found sleeping together on twigs too!

> ***Location:*** *Throughout Australia.*

### TEDDY BEAR BEE
*Amegilla bombiformis* v

Teddy bear bees get their name from their golden-brown setae that resembles fur. These bees are solitary and dig out nests in soil, where they create urn-shaped cells. These nest cells are stocked with a care package of nectar and pollen for each baby bee. A single egg is laid in each cell and the young bee larva feeds on this sugar and protein package until it is ready to pupate, then emerge as an adult bee.

> ***Location:*** *Throughout the east coast of Australia.*

# CUCKOO BEES
## TRIBE MELECTINI

### NEON CUCKOO BEE
*Thyreus nitidulus* ^

Neon cuckoo bees are some of the loveliest looking solitary bees you will find in Australia or New Guinea. Do not let their charms mislead you though, they have a dark life history. These bees parasitise the nests of the poor blue-banded bees by laying their egg inside the other bee's nest!

> ***Location:*** *Coastal regions of Darwin, Queensland, New South Wales, and Victoria.*

# CARPENTER BEES
## SUBFAMILY XYLOCOPINAE

### GIANT CARPENTER BEE
*Xylocopa aruana* <

Giant carpenter bees are the largest bees in Australia. All carpenter bees are solitary. These bees excavate burrows out of soft timber and create a nest inside. They can reuse old nests each year and often make new nests in the same site. They divide their nests into multiple sections and provision each with pollen and a single egg. The females are yellow and black, a form of warning colouration, while males are golden brown.

^ ***Location:*** *Coastal areas of the Northern Territory, Queensland, New South Wales, and northern Western Australia.*

# PLASTERER BEES FAMILY COLLETIDAE

### CLOUDY MASKED BEE
*Hylaeus nubilosus* >

The cloudy masked bee is a small bee that can use abandoned nests of mud wasps as its own nest. It can be commonly found in backyards and at bee hotels. This species is native to eastern Australia but has more recently been moved into Western Australia.

> ***Location:*** *Coastal regions of Queensland, New South Wales, Victoria, Tasmania, and Western Australia.*

### BLUE MASKED BEE
*Palaeorhiza* sp. ∨

These small native bees feed on the nectar and delicate pollen of gum flowers. The pollen serves as a source of protein for the bees and helps them lay more eggs. These bees resemble wasps, but close inspection of their bodies reveals the fine hairs or setae covering their body and unique wing venation.

> ***Location:*** *Coastal Queensland and northern New South Wales.*

# LEAFCUTTER BEES
## FAMILY MEGACHILIDAE

### GOLDEN-FRONTED RESIN BEE
*Megachile aurifrons* >

The golden-fronted resin bee makes its own resin out of chewed up leaves. These bees make their nests in hollow stems or old mud wasp nests. They can often be seen covered in pollen, which gathers on their abdomen. The bees make a pollen-paste to feed their larvae. Female bees have red eyes, and will lay a single egg in each cell of their nest, then cap it off with their leaf-resin.

> ***Location:*** *Throughout Australia, except Tasmania.*

Bees work hard to make their nests.

They have to defend their nest from other bees and wasps that can steal or parasitise their nest.

### FIRE TAILED RESIN BEE
*Megachile mystaceana* ∧

The fire tailed resin bee has a bright orange-red abdomen that contrasts with the rest of its black body. It cuts out discs from leaves and uses these to line its nest in existing holes, like hollow stems, or rock crevices. Leaf-cutter bees like this species also have long tongues that they use to feed on flowers with difficult to access nectar.

> ***Location:*** *Coastal Queensland and New South Wales.*

# WASPS

Wasps' diversity is suspected to be large because we know that for most insects, there is a parasitic wasp that attacks it. Most wasps are very small, as they can parasitise eggs and other life stages of insects. This makes them challenging to study, so we need more taxonomists who can study them and describe the remaining species!

**PARASITIC WASPS**

## GASTERUPTION WASP

### FAMILY GASTERUPTIIDAE

Gasteruption wasps parasitise solitary bee nests. Once the bees supplied all the needed food for their larvae, they will seal off the chamber. The gasteruption wasp inspects these nests while the bee is away, and will use her long ovipositor to lay eggs in the nest. Overtime, the wasp larvae eats the food provided by the mother-bee and then it eats the bee larvae!

> ***Location:*** *Coastal regions throughout Australia.*

## PERILAMPID WASPS

### FAMILY PERILAMPIDAE

Perilampid wasps are a special kind of parasite. These tiny wasps attack other parasites like tachinid flies! When the tachinid fly parasitises a caterpillar, the fly is then parasitised by this wasp. Later on, the wasp emerges from the fly inside the caterpillar! This is called hyperparasitism.

> ***Location:*** *Coastal regions of Queensland, New South Wales, Victoria, Tasmania, and South Australia.*

## BEE-PARASITE WASP

### FAMILY LEUCOSPIDAE

Leucospid wasps parasitise the nests of solitary bees by unhinging their abdomen, unfolding an ovipositor, and then drilling through the sealed nest of the bee. After they lay an egg in the nest, the wasp larva hatches out and eats the bee larva. The young wasp can then safely develop in the chamber prepared by the bee. Because of this relationship, these wasps can often be seen around bee hotels. They can be shy and easily sacred away as they must sneakily parasitise the bee nest. If caught, the solitary bee may attack the wasp. These wasps also mimic the appearance of social paper wasps, but they cannot sting people!

> ***Location:*** *Coastal regions throughout Australia.*

# FIG WASPS

## FAMILY AGAONIDAE

Fig wasps have a close relationship with fig trees. The flowers of these trees are inside unripened figs, but they need to be pollinated. Female fig wasps crawl into unripened figs using their wedge-shaped head. The wasps lose their wings in this process, but once inside the fig, they pollinate some of the flowers! The wasp also lays her eggs in specialised fig flowers. These young fig wasps then develop as the fig ripens but getting out of a fig is just as difficult as getting inside of it! Thankfully, male fig wasps are specially adapted for this. The males will emerge inside of the fig first. They fertilise the female wasps and then chew an exit hole so the females can easily escape the fig. Before the females leave, they collect pollen from their home fig, and carry this to the next fig to continue the pollination.

Male fig wasps have an important part to play.

Both pollinating and parasitising fig wasps can be found within a single fig.

^ ***Location:*** *Coastal regions throughout Australia.*

### FACT

Most figs are pollinated by wasps, and if you find one without any holes, you will likely see tiny wasps inside. Figs that are sold at the grocery store are a unique variety that do not require pollination to ripen, so there are no wasps inside them!

# FIG WASP PARASITOIDS

Parasitic fig wasps have long ovipositors that look like tails. These ovipositors drill through the fig to lay eggs inside.

## FAMILIES TORYMIDAE & PTEROMALIDAE

Other wasps have taken advantage of the unique relationship between figs and fig wasps. Once the fig wasp has laid its eggs inside the fig, another group of wasps with long ovipositors drill through the flesh of the fig to lay their own eggs inside. This second group of wasps are a special kind of parasite that use a host, like the fig wasp to feed on, but they kill their host as they grow! We call these deadly parasites 'parasitoids'. These parasitoid wasps cannot kill all the fig wasps though! The parasitoids still need some fig wasps to survive as the male pollinating fig wasps chew exit holes that the parasitoids rely on to escape from the fig.

> ***Location:*** *Coastal regions throughout Australia.*

# CUCKOO WASPS

## SUPERFAMILY CHRYSIDOIDEA

### CUCKOO WASP

*Primeuchroeus* sp. >

Much like a cuckoo bird, cuckoo wasps parasitise the nests of others. In this case, the wasp lays its eggs in the nests of solitary bees. Some bees will fill a nesting cavity with food for their larva, then seal the chamber. The cuckoo wasp takes advantage of the bee's hard work and sneakily lays its egg in the bee's nest. The wasp larva will then eat the food provided by the bee and then eat the bee's larva! This type of parasite is called a cleptoparasite, or 'stealing' parasite.

> ***Location:*** *Throughout Australia, but poorly documented.*

Cuckoo wasps must be sneaky and quick.

Solitary bees have to guard their nests from parasitic wasps like the cuckoo wasp.

**DARWIN WASPS**

SUPERFAMILY ICHNEUMONOIDEA

# ICHNEUMONID WASPS

## FAMILY ICHNEUMONIDAE

### DIADEGMA WASP

*Diadegma semiclausum* >

Some parasitic wasps are useful for managing pests of our crops. One example is the Diadegma wasp which parasitises the diamondback moth (*Plutella xylostella*). The wasp attacks the caterpillars of this moth, laying an egg inside of the larva. Instead of developing into a moth, parasitised caterpillars will later emerge as wasps. This provides a natural pest control option to combat pests that damage our crops. These wasps are also host-specific, meaning they can only parasitise the diamondback moth.

> ***Location:*** *Cabbage and broccoli farms throughout Australia.*

### PROCESS OF PARASITISM

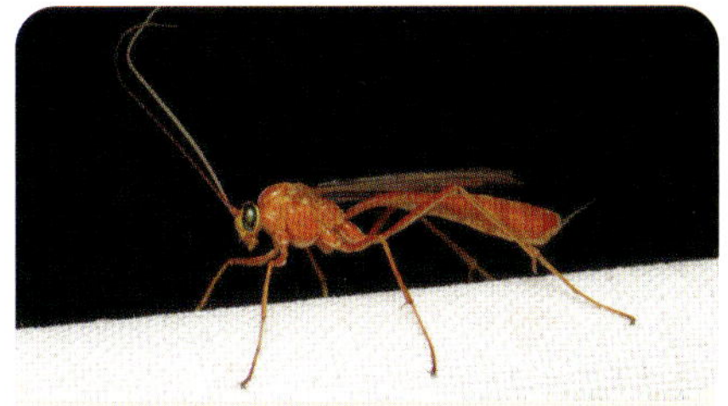

### ORANGE DARWIN WASP

*Netelia* sp. ^

These wasps paralyse caterpillars with their sting and then lay an egg near the caterpillar's head. When the wasp larva hatches, it feeds on the caterpillar, but it does not kill it. Instead, the caterpillar develops with the wasp! Once the caterpillar has grown large enough to pupate, it will prepare a chamber in the soil. At this point, the wasp kills the caterpillar and uses the pupation chamber for itself!

> ***Location:*** *Coastal regions of Tasmania, South Australia, Western Australia, Queensland, New South Wales and Victoria.*

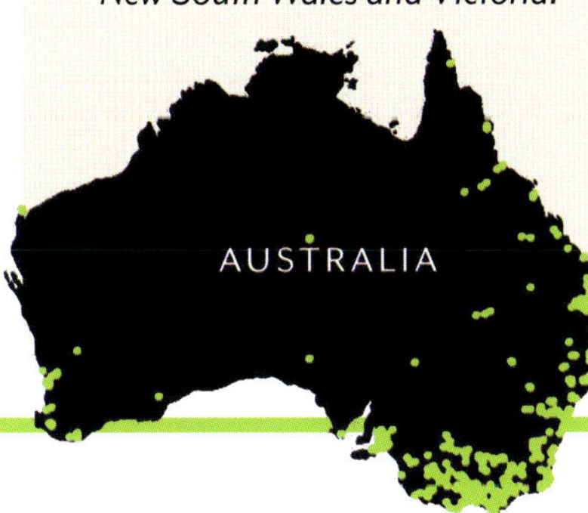

# BRACONID WASPS

## FAMILY BRACONIDAE

### GIANT WOOD MOTH PARASITOID WASP

*Virgulibracon endoxylaphagus* <

The giant wood moth parasitoid wasp is a large pink and black wasp with one of the longest ovipositors or stingers recorded. They keep their long ovipositor in a protective black sheath until they are ready to parasitise the larva of the giant wood moth. Caterpillars of this moth live in deep tunnels inside the trunks or branches of gum trees. The only way that these wasps can access the caterpillars is to drill through the tree with their long ovipositor! This process can take hours and several wasps can be seen trying to parasitise one large, hidden caterpillar.

> ***Location:*** *This species likely occurs throughout the distribution of the giant wood moth, but is currently only known from southeast Queensland.*

**VESPID WASPS**

SUPERFAMILY VESPIOIDEA

# PAPER WASPS

## FAMILY VESPIDAE

**PAPER WASPS CAN RECOGNISE EACH OTHER!**

They have unique patterns on their faces and this allows the social wasps to recognise which wasps have been helping and which have not. This allows wasps to get rid of free-loading individuals who benefit from, but do not help the nest.

### STICK-NEST BROWN PAPER WASP

*Ropalidia revolutionalis* >

Paper wasps live in family groups that build long, multi-celled nests out of paper. You can find them collecting materials for this on wood or tree bark. By living in a group, the wasps can share duties of the nest which include building the nest, feeding their larvae, and guarding the nest from predators and parasitoids.

> ***Location:*** *Coastal regions of Queensland and New South Wales.*

**Photograph:** Bridgette Gower

# SPIDER WASPS

## FAMILY POMPILIDAE

Spider wasps have some of the most painful stings. This is because their sting is used to paralyse spider prey. Once a wasp has paralysed a spider, it will drag the spider to a burrow. Here, it lays an egg on the spider and closes the burrow. Over time, that egg hatches into a wasp larva that eats the spider as it develops. The spider is not dead though, only paralysed during this process, which keeps the food fresh for the young wasp. By the next season, an adult wasp will emerge from the burrow and hunt for her own spider prey.

> ***Location:*** *Throughout Australia.*

# VELVET ANTS

## FAMILY MUTILLIDAE

Velvet ants aren't ants at all! They are actually wasps!

**Photograph:** Dr. Andrew Maynard.

### GREEN VELVET ANT

*Ephutomorpha princeps* <

Velvet ants are actually wingless wasps! This group of predators advertises the painful sting of the females with bright colours. When they find a bee or wasp larva in a nest, they will parasitise it by laying an egg on the larva. Male velvet ants have wings to fly to the female and can be mistaken for another species.

> ***Location:*** *Throughout Australia.*

# MUD WASPS

## FAMILY SPHECIDAE

### VASE-CELL MUD-DAUBER WASP

*Sceliphron formosum* >

Vase-cell mud-dauber wasps are one of many wasps that construct nests out of mud. These pill-shaped nests are built up mouthful by mouthful of mud collected by the wasp. Once constructed, the female will fill the nest with spiders and lay a single egg inside each nest. The spiders are paralysed and will be food for the wasp's larva inside the cell. The larva then pupates inside of this nest, making a silken pupal case within. It then emerges the next year as an adult.

### MUD WASP LIFECYCLE

> *Location: Coastal regions of Queensland, New South Wales, Victoria, South Australia, and Western Australia.*

# FLOWER WASPS

## FAMILY THYNNIDAE

Female flower wasps are wingless and nearly blind. They spend most of their lives as a parasite of beetles or other invertebrates in the soil. Once they are ready to mate, they hitch onto a male, which is winged with fully developed eyes. This pair will remain attached as the male transports the female to flowers to feed. Once the mating has finished, females burrow back into the soil, to lay an egg on a new host.

> ***Location:*** *Throughout Australia, primarily coastal regions.*

CHAPTER 3

# ANTS AND SAWFLIES

## SUBORDER APOCRITA AND SYMPHYTA

Weaver ants stitch leaves together using silk from their larvae.

# INTRODUCTION

Ants and sawflies make up the other groups within Order Hymenoptera. Ants are more closely related to bees and wasps, with their narrow waist, social structure, and stings. Sawflies, however, are more like an ancient version of ants, bees, and wasps. Sawflies do not have a narrow waist, cannot sting, and are often found in groups as larvae, but are not truly social.

Ants live in social colonies where a queen lays eggs and worker ants take care of the larvae and forage for food.

The queen and her workers are female, and males are only produced when a new queen is made. Males are produced from unfertilised eggs and only live for a short time when they try to mate with a new queen. Queens will store sperm from this single mating event for the rest of their lives and use it to fertilise all their eggs.

Elbowed antennae

Node between the thorax and the abdomen

ANT

Bottlebrush sawfly adult. **Photograph:** Lauren Wade.

## FACT

Ants communicate through smells! Their antennae are sensitive to a variety of scents allowing them to recognise their sisters, find food, and follow pheromone trails.

Queen ant

Only male ants and new queens have wings. After mating, queen ants will lose their wings, typically by chewing them off.

## WORKER ANTS

The worker ants also defend the nest, with some ant species having specialised defence workers called soldier or major ants. The soldiers often have larger bodies and heads with big mandibles or jaws. The workers of the colony cannot lay eggs and depend on the queen to reproduce. The ants work like cells of a body and are considered eusocial or truly social animals.

## SAWFLIES

Female sawflies have a saw-like ovipositor that they use to cut open plant tissue before laying their egg. This is how they got their name!

# ANTS
FAMILY FORMICIDAE

# BULLDOG AND JUMPER ANTS
SUBFAMILY MYRMECIINAE

LONGEST ANT IN AUSTRALIA

## GIANT BULL ANT
*Myrmecia brevinoda* <

This giant of the ant world builds deep nest galleries with concealed entrances and a mound at the top. All bull ants (*Myrmecia* spp.) are known for their painful sting. They lock onto prey with their long, serrated jaws and hold it in position to be stung by the tip of their abdomen. The sting kills or paralyses an insect, making it easier to take back to their nest. Worker ants gather food items like this to feed the larvae in their nest, while adults have delicate mouthparts between their large jaws to feed on nectar and sap flows.

> ***Location:*** *East coast of Australia.*

## JUMPING JACK ANT
*Myrmecia nigrocincta* ^

The jumping jack ant is best known for its ability to jump over relatively long distances. This ant can jump 10cm! That's over six times its body length, the equivalent of a person jumping over 10m! These ants forage in trees where jumping comes in handy for navigating. They are omnivores, feeding on insects and nectar from flowers. Since they visit gum flowers (*Eucalyptus* spp.) and carry some pollen away, these ants are considered pollinators.

v ***Location:*** *East coast of Australia, including Queensland, New South Wales, Victoria, and South Australia.*

**FACT**

**Unlike other worker ants, bull ant workers can lay eggs! This means if their queen dies, the worker ants can step in to keep the colony going.**

## RED BULL ANT
*Myrmecia gulosa* >

This ant is also one of the largest in Australia, with some ants being 3cm long. This species is considered to be more primitive because they struggle to cooperate in large social groups like other ants. These ants are typically spotted hunting or foraging on their own. Adult ants feed on liquid as their large jaws are only used for catching prey. The ants will carry an insect back to their nest and the meat of the prey is fed to their larvae. Like all bull ants, this species has well-developed eyes. They use this vision to stalk prey, but if you watch them, they may watch you back!

> ***Location:*** *Southeast Queensland and New South Wales.*

Be careful around bull ants! Each species has a painful sting.

# BLACK TREE AND GREEN ANTS

## SUBFAMILIES PSEUDOMYRMECINAE AND ECTATOMMINAE

This strange, long ant forages alone on gum trees.

### BLACK TREE ANT

*Tetraponera punctulata* ^

This unique, long black ant is common through most coastal areas of Australia. This species nests in the dead branches of trees, usually eucalypts. They can often be found in the old homes of wood-boring beetles or moths, and often farm scale insects. Scale insects produce a sugary liquid called honeydew that the ants feed on. Their generalist diet allows them to occupy several different areas.

> **Location:** *Coastal areas of the Northern Territory, Queensland, New South Wales, Victoria, and Western Australia.*

The metallic greens and blues of these ants may help them blend in!

### GREEN-HEADED ANT

*Rhytidoponera metallica* ^

These ants are most known for their painful sting. They are small, metallic green to blue ants, which actively forage both in natural habitats and many urban areas. The worker ants search for other invertebrates which they sting to subdue, and then carry back to their nest to feed to the ant larvae. Worker ants can also collect seeds to eat. The ants will bury many seeds as they collect them, and often bury more than they need. When fires come through a landscape, some of these buried seeds germinate, making the ants an unexpected gardener.

> **Location:** *Every state except Tasmania.*

# MYRMICINE ANTS

## SUBFAMILY MYRMICINAE

### MUSCLE MAN ANTS

*Podomyrma odae* >

Muscle man ants are easily recognised by their swollen femora or legs that make the ants look like they have large muscles. These ants live in and often forage in trees. They can make their nests in the old tunnels of wood-boring insects like the giant wood moth. During the day, these ants will forage all alone.

> **Location:** *Coastal regions of Queensland and New South Wales.*

THE LONE FORAGER

# SPINY AND SUGAR ANTS

## SUBFAMILY FORMICINAE

FACT

Honey pot ants have been consumed by Indigenous Australians for thousands of years and are very important to their culture and survival in the desert.

Photograph: Mitsuhiko Imamori – Minden Pictures.

### GOLDEN TAILED SPINY ANTS

*Polyrhachis ammon* ^

The golden tailed spiny ant is one of several species of spiny ants that has metallic gold colouration. These colours may help the ant reflect the heat from the sun as they forage in open eucalypt habitats. Spiny ants get their name from the large spines found on the backs or mesosomas of most species.

> ***Location:*** *Open eucalypt forests of Tropical North Queensland, New South Wales and Victoria.*

### SUGAR ANTS

*Camponotus* spp. ^

There are over 100 species of sugar ants in Australia and each species can be very abundant. These ants can nest under rocks or bark and in tree hollows. They are named after their attraction to sugar and farming practices. Yes, ants can farm. These ants will harvest honeydew produced by bugs like aphids and scale insects. The ants will move these bugs to new plants and guard the bugs from predators.

> ***Location:*** *Throughout all of Australia.*

### AUSTRALIAN HONEY POT ANTS

*Camponotus inflatus* ^

Several different species of ants are called honey pot ants. This comes from each species having a special caste called a replete. Repletes are a special type of worker ant that is fed large amounts of honeydew by their sisters when there is plenty of food. The repletes then store this food to regurgitate and feed their sisters throughout the year.

> ***Location:*** *Desert regions of Western Australia, the Northern Territory and South Australia.*

### WEAVER ANTS OR GREEN TREE ANTS

*Oecophylla smaragdina* >

Weaver ants build large nests out of the leaves of trees. They do this by pulling the leaves together with worker ants, while another worker uses an ant larva to produce silk and fasten the leaves together. In a way, the ant larva functions as a hot glue gun for these ants. No, adult ants cannot produce silk, but ant larvae can make silk to prepare a safe chamber to pupate in. The use of this silk has allowed the weaver ants to make a nest wherever they choose, and the ants can be found nesting in plants in tropical regions.

Weaver ants farm bugs for their honeydew.

> ***Location:*** *Northern regions of Western Australia, the Northern Territory, and Queensland.*

### RATTLE ANTS

*Polyrhachis australis* ^

This species builds its nests in trees and shrubs by weaving together leaves. The leaves are attached using silk and debris. Like the weaver ants, rattle ants use the silk produced by their larvae to stitch together their arboreal nest. If disturbed, the nest will rattle like a maraca as the ants inside hurry outside.

> ***Location:*** *Rainforests of Queensland and New South Wales.*

# PONY ANTS

## SUBFAMILY PONERINAE

### TRAP JAW ANTS

*Odontomachus* spp. >

**CLEVER!**
Trap jaw ants have a special escape technique.

The trap jaw ant can snap its jaws closed in a flash!

Trap jaw ants forage for food with their jaws wide open. These jaws are locked open in preparation for two events: catching prey or escaping danger. When released, the jaws snap shut instantly. This can be used to catch quick prey, but if the jaws are directed downwards when they snap close, they can also send the ant spiralling away! This is useful when the ant needs a quick escape. Jaws are not the only weapon these ants have, trap jaw ants fully subdue their prey by stinging them. This species often lives in leaf litter and hunts termites. Once it has trapped and stung a termite, it carries it back to the nest to feed to its larvae. Trap jaw ant larvae are covered in spikes to prevent them from mistaking each other for a termite-meal.

> **Location:** *Throughout Australia.*

# MEAT ANTS

## SUBFAMILY DOLICHODERINAE

Meat ants will rush outside if you get too close to their nest!

### GIANT MEAT ANTS

*Iridomyrmex purpureus* ^

This species nests in wide, semi-flat mounds of sand and pebbles. Sandy, clear paths leading to the nest can be made by the hundreds of worker ants that forage for food. These large ants are also very aggressive and if you walk by their nest, several worker ants will pour out, ready to attack. The worker ants are often eaten by birds and other animals. By coming out in such large numbers, the ants can help protect one another from these predators. These ants can also secrete smelly formic acid from their pygidial gland on the end of their abdomen.

> **Location:** *Every state except Tasmania.*

### RED SPIDER ANTS

*Leptomyrmex rufipes* v

Spider ants fold their abdomens over their bodies when they forage for food. This distorts their body shape, making them look more like spiders than ants. This species can live in rainforests or open eucalypt forests, showing that they can survive in a variety of conditions. They often nest near the ground in live trees or under logs.

> **Location:** *Coast of Queensland and northern New South Wales.*

**FACT**
Spider ants have repletes that store honey for the ant colony. When they are too full of honey, they cannot escape the nest and instead hang from the ceiling.

# INVASIVE ANTS

Photograph: François Brassard.

**Photograph:** Alamy.

## RED IMPORTED FIRE ANTS

*Solenopsis invicta*

Fire ants are named after their painful, burning sting. They are small ants that make dome-shaped nests in soils. If you accidentally disturb one of their nests, you will quickly find yourself covered with angry little ants! Fire ants are originally from South America but have become a major invasive pest here in Australia. Aside from the pain they cause to people, they also harm our native wildlife. Thankfully, there is a national fire ant eradication program to help manage this invasive ant.

> ***Location:*** *Currently only found in southeast Queensland, originally from South America.*

**Photograph:** François Brassard.

Crazy ants live up to their name.

## YELLOW CRAZY ANTS

*Anoplolepis gracilipes*

Yellow crazy ants were first detected in northern Queensland in 2011, but no one is sure of their specific origin. These ants are highly invasive and have caused the most destruction on Christmas Island where the Christmas Island pipistrelle, a local bat, has since gone extinct. These ants can grow to large numbers because they have supercolonies. Instead of having individual colonies that each have their own queen, this species has large, interconnected nests with multiple queens. This allows them to outcompete other ant species. The destruction of this ant extends beyond the ant world, however. These crazy ants feed on other invertebrates and small animals like frogs and nesting birds. Efforts by scientists to remove this ant are critical to protecting our native animals.

**FACT**

**These ants do not have a stinger, but they can spray formic acid. When they attack, they spray this acid and can blind animals like birds, turtles, and crabs.**

> ***Location:*** *The Northern Territory, Christmas Island, and Queensland.*

## ELECTRIC ANTS

*Wasmannia auropunctata*

ELECTRIFYING STING!

Electric ants get their name from their painful sting which feels like an electric shock! These small ants can nest in a variety of substrates from potting soil and sugar cane mulch to exposed logs and rocks. This nesting versatility has helped them colonise items which have been imported overseas, so when goods were brought over, these ants were accidentally introduced as well. They are a major concern due to the pain they cause humans and their destructive impact on other animals including insects, birds, and turtles. These ants are known to sting the eyes of large animals, blinding them.

> ***Location:*** *Currently only found in Tropical North Queensland, originally from Central and South America.*

**Photograph:** Alex Wild.

# SAWFLIES FAMILY PERGIDAE

## LONG-TAILED SAWFLIES

### SUBFAMILY PTERYGOPHORINAE

#### THE DYING MOTHER SAWFLY

*Pteryperga galla* ↘

Females of this species will lay their eggs on the young leaves of blueberry ash trees (*Eleaocarpus reticulatus*) and then stand guard over them until they die. The guarding mother protects the eggs from being parasitised and the newly hatched larvae from predators.

> **Location:** *Coastal areas of Queensland and New South Wales.*

#### GREEN LONG-TAILED SAWFLY

*Lophyrotoma* spp. <

This species' larvae feed on the leaves of paperbark trees (*Melaleuca* spp.) and this has become useful to scientists who are trying to manage these trees overseas.

> **Location:** *Several species throughout coastal regions of Australia, except for the Northern Territory.*

**Photograph:** Lauren Wade.

#### BOTTLEBRUSH SAWFLY

*Pterygophorus cinctus* ^

Bottlebrush sawfly larvae devour the leaves of bottlebrush or paperbark trees (*Melaleuca* spp.), while adults feed on the nectar from flowers. The larvae will feed in groups when they are young, but as they grow larger and eat more, they must feed in smaller groups or alone. The pupae of this species are also strangely naked, making no cocoon to protect themselves during this vulnerable phase.

> **Location:** *Coastal regions of Queensland, New South Wales, Victoria, Tasmania, and South Australia.*

## SPITFIRES SUBFAMILY PERGINAE

Sawflies are more frequently encountered when they are still larvae. These sawfly larvae feed on the leaves of eucalypts and can eat all the leaves of a small sapling. Once they have eaten all the leaves on one plant, they will crawl in a cluster to the next tree, usually in the late afternoon or evening. By sticking together in large numbers, sawflies can help protect one another from predators and any potential parasitoids like tachinid flies. But numbers are not their only defence. When disturbed, each sawfly will rear up its head and the end of its body. It will hold a bubble of vomit in its mouth and a thick yellow nub of condensed eucalyptus oil on its rear end, which it waves around.

> **Location:** *Throughout Australia.*

These larvae are armed against predators with bubbles of vomit.

CHAPTER 4

# FLIES

## ORDER DIPTERA

Several flies are important pollinators as adults, while their larvae have different feeding habits. For instance, the larvae of this hoverfly feed on aphids and can help farmers manage pest outbreaks!

## INTRODUCTION

Insects are typically defined by the species that we most frequently encounter. In this case, the flies we see most often are pests of some sort. Mosquitoes, midges, and March flies bite us and suck our blood, leaving itchy bumps. Fly larvae are also known as maggots, which can be found feeding in rotting organisms like fungi, dead animals, and old food, or even fresh produce like the fruit flies which may ruin our perfect harvests. But here you'll learn how flies have been poorly judged by most. Flies are some of the most important pollinators and nutrient recyclers. Their role in the natural world is irreplaceable and some of them can be quite beautiful.

Flies are one of the most diverse groups of insects with over 120,000 species described!

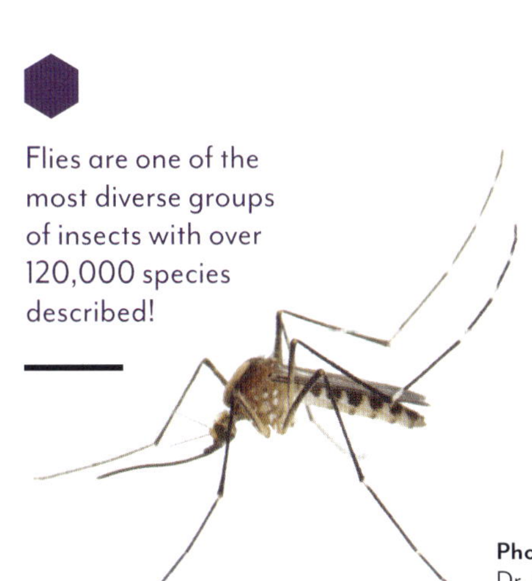

**FLIES CANNOT STING,** but some species have a painful bite!

**Photograph:** Dr. Andrew Maynard.

### MOLLUSC ANT HOVERFLY

*Paramixogaster* sp. <

Flies can be identified by their single set of wings. The order name, Diptera is from Greek words for 'two wings.' Instead of having hindwings, flies have a set of halteres which mildly resemble chicken drumsticks. These halteres help flies with their balance in flight, making them very agile fliers. The mouthparts of flies are adapted for piercing and sucking, as seen in mosquitoes, or for lapping and sucking on fluids, like that of a fruit fly or hover fly.

# BLOWFLIES FAMILY CALLIPHORIDAE

## YELLOW-HEADED SNAIL PARASITIC BLOWFLY

*Amenia imperialis* <

The snail parasitic blowfly is a very beautiful metallic-coloured fly, but as their common name suggests, they have a parasitic stage that isn't so charming. These blowflies are unique in that they give birth to live larvae. Instead of laying eggs as most insects do, these flies have each egg hatch inside their body. The first instar larvae then develop inside the mother fly's uterus until they reach their much larger, second larval instar and are equipped with mandibular hooks (hooks around the mouth). At this stage they enter the world, and likely their snail host. A number of these flies have been reared from snails, but few details are known about their biology and their interaction with their snail hosts.

**FACT**

**These flies give live birth to an enormous larva! Because this larva is so big, females can often only have one baby at a time.**

∨ *Location: Coastal regions of Queensland, New South Wales, and Victoria.*

# BEE FLIES FAMILY BOMBYLIIDAE

Bee flies are important pollinators in a variety of ecosystems and are often mistaken for bees given their appearance and hovering flight. Their fluffy bodies easily collect pollen as they visit flowers. Some bee flies, such as the Compto bee fly (*Comptosia sp.*) are also known to mate on hilltops. Males will fight each other with spines on their wings to dominate these hilltops and each site is used for multiple generations! This sort of behaviour is also seen in birds but is surprising to see in an insect.

**Bee fly emerging from a wasp's nest.**

Some female bee flies have a special chamber on their abdomen to collect sand grains! They use this sand as a coating to protect their eggs.

## FLUFFY BLACK BEE FLY

*Nigromyia* sp. >

> ***Location:*** *Coastal regions of Western Australia, the Northern Territory, and Queensland.*

## BANDED BEE FLY

*Villa* sp. ∨

This species demonstrates the mimicry of bees found in this group. These flies resemble bees or wasps, with yellow bands warning any potential predators that this insect may sting when it actually cannot. At night, these flies can be found sleeping on the ends of twigs and if disturbed, they will return to the same place to continue their rest.

> ***Location:*** *Throughout coastal regions of Australia, except the Northern Territory.*

# BRISTLE FLIES

## FAMILY TACHINIDAE

Several adult flies feed on nectar and pollen.

### RUTILIA FLIES

*Rutilia* spp. >

The shiny metallic colours of these flies may make them difficult to spot for predators. Their lovely appearance as adults disguises their parasitic nature as larvae. Several species of Rutilia flies parasitise the larvae of scarab beetles. The larvae can enter the body of a beetle larva and remain there, growing slowly inside the live grub until it is close to pupating. Instead of becoming a beetle pupa, a large fly pupa will emerge. Adult flies of this group can frequently be seen feeding on flowers or sunning themselves on gum trees, typically with their head pointed down.

> ***Location:*** *Throughout Australia.*

# FRUIT FLIES

## FAMILY TEPHRITIDAE

### QUEENSLAND FRUIT FLY

*Bactrocera tryoni*

Queensland fruit flies are native to Australia, but wreak havoc on our crops. They lay their eggs in the flesh of fruits and their larvae will then feed inside the fruit, making it rot and often drop early. You can spot fruit fly damage when a fruit begins to develop large bruises with tissue that is soft to the touch. All of a farmer's fruit can be destroyed by an infestation of these flies, leading entomologists to study the species in order to develop safe and novel ways to manage this native pest.

**FACT**

**This fly is estimated to cost $28.5 million a year in damage to Australian crops!**

^ ***Location:*** *Coastal regions of Queensland, New South Wales, Victoria, and South Australia.*

### CUCUMBER FRUIT FLY

*Zeugodacus cucumis* ^

Like the Queensland fruit fly, this species is native to Australia and causes damage to several crops. It is most known for its damage to cucumbers, but it also lays its eggs in papayas, passionfruit, and several other crops.

> ***Location:*** *Coastal areas of the Northern Territory, Queensland, and northern New South Wales.*

# FUNGUS GNATS

## FAMILY KEROPLATIDAE

### GLOW WORMS
*Arachnocampa* spp. >

Like stars in the night sky, these glowing 'worms' illuminate the dark corners of moist caves and rainforest gullies in Australia and New Zealand. These are not true worms though, instead they are the larval stage of a fly called a fungus gnat. Calling these insects glow maggots just does not have the same appeal. Each glow worm drops several lines of silk called snares, which are beaded with mucus. They then glow from the end of their body and this light attracts other insects, which get caught in the sticky snares. If you explore these areas at night, you may see their magical blue lights. Otherwise, you can visit caves that are famous for these glow worms.

Glow worms from the genus Arachnocampa are only found in Australia and New Zealand! There are many other types of bioluminescent insects that are also commonly called 'glow worms', including the larvae of beetles.

Adult glow worm

Photograph: Dr. Dave Merritt.

Glow worms lure in prey with their bioluminescent bums!

Photograph: Julia Marr.

### YELLOW -SHOULDERED HOVER FLY
*Simosyrphus grandicornis* ⌄

This species is one of the most common hoverflies in Australia, but it can also be found in the Pacific Islands. Adult flies look like small bees or wasps, but flies cannot sting. They feed on the nectar from a variety of native and introduced flowers. On some farms, these hoverflies are considered important for managing pests. This is because the flies will lay their eggs near clusters of aphids. Once their larvae hatch, the hoverfly maggot will eat the aphids, naturally controlling the pest.

> ***Location:*** *Throughout Australia.*

# HOVERFLIES

## FAMILY SYRPHIDAE

### MOLLUSC ANT FLY
*Paramixogaster* spp. >

This group is called ant flies (Subfamily Microdontinae) because their larvae live inside ant nests and feed on the ants' larvae. These fly larvae do not look like typical maggots, but instead resemble a mollusc. Their strange appearance is thought to function more for protection or disguise than for mimicry. The ants cannot bite or sting this well-defended intruder, and the fly larva spends most of its life in the ant nest. The larva breathes through a stump called a respiratory process on its rear end. Once the larva has pupated, two spiracles appear near its head, which also help it breathe. The adult fly later emerges from this strange dome, breaking the head section into three pieces. As adults, they resemble wasps and bees and this is thought to be an example of mimicry as the flies are likely given protection by resembling other insects with the ability to sting.

⌄ ***Location:*** *Coastal regions of every state except the Northern Territory.*

Pupa

# MOSQUITOES

## FAMILY CULICIDAE

Mosquitoes begin their lives in water! This means that without water, there are no mosquitoes. Their larvae can live in fresh or saltwater and prefer standing pools where they may graze for food. Adult mosquitoes are most known for biting humans and transferring deadly pathogens like malaria and dengue, but very few species are capable of this. In fact, out of over 300 mosquito species in Australia, only a dozen pose a risk to humans.

**Photograph:** Dr. Andrew Maynard.

**FACT**

**Mosquitoes are the deadliest animals on the planet! They transmit pathogens which kill millions of people each year.**

### FROG-LOVING MOSQUITO

*Uranotaenia* spp.

Not all mosquitoes bite humans, some prefer to feed on other animals like frogs! This species can be caught by playing frog calls and emitting carbon dioxide, the two cues that it uses to find its frog-meals. For the most part, these mosquitoes do not have a harmful impact on the frog, but they can transfer parasitic roundworms to the frog that can cause illnesses. The larvae of these mosquitoes can survive in a wide range of habitats from freshwater ponds to brackish swamps.

> ***Location:*** *Coastal areas of North Western Australia, the Northern Territory, Queensland, and New South Wales.*

**Photograph:** Stephen Zozaya.

Other species of elephant mosquitoes have been trialled in some parts of the world to control dengue outbreaks. This is because their larvae can eat the larvae of disease-vectoring mosquitoes.

### ELEPHANT MOSQUITO

*Toxorhynchites speciosus*

These giant, colourful mosquitoes do not feed on blood. Instead, they feed on nectar. The larvae, or wrigglers, live in standing water and eat the wrigglers of other mosquitoes, including pest species. This helps make the elephant mosquito larger than most mosquitoes. It is also part of why this species does not need to feed on blood as an adult, as the protein required to produce eggs is gained during their voracious larval stage. They are common in urban areas and often breed in water held in the leaves of garden bromeliads. Instead of landing to lay their eggs, this species fires them individually into pools of water while flying. If you find one, you can thank it personally for keeping populations of pest mosquitoes in check.

> ***Location:*** *Coastal regions of the Northern Territory, Queensland, and New South Wales.*

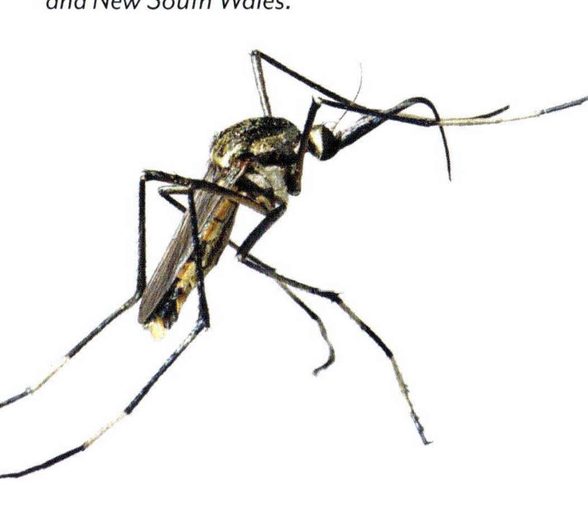

Photograph by: Dr. Andrew Maynard.

## IN-YOUR-FACE MOSQUITO

*Tripteroides atripes* >

This species is most common in the southern states of Australia, where it breeds in both natural and artificial water containers. They often bite people and fly around the face and nose before landing. It is not known why they have this peculiar habit, but we can pretend they fly around our faces because they want to let us know they are there. Or perhaps they like the smell of carbon dioxide coming out of our mouths and noses. Thankfully, this species is not considered a health risk.

> **Location:** *Coastal and inland regions of Queensland, New South Wales, Victoria, Tasmania and South Australia.*

Only female mosquitoes need a blood-meal, so they are the only ones that bite!

**FACT**
The larvae of this species gain their oxygen directly from plants!

## ORANGE SWAMP MOSQUITO

*Coquillettidia xanthogaster* ^

This medium-sized mosquito is common around freshwater wetlands with lots of vegetation. They are easily recognised due to their bright orange colour and unique scales. Their larvae have a modified siphon at the end of their abdomen which they plug into plants to gain oxygen. Adult females often bite people and can transfer harmful viruses like Ross River, which is the most common mosquito-borne infection in Australia. Here, a female of this species can be seen biting the author who was otherwise distracted by photographing insects.

> **Location:** *Coastal and inland areas of Western Australia, the Northern Territory, Queensland, and New South Wales.*

# MARCH OR HORSE FLIES

## FAMILY TABANIDAE

### GOLDEN BUSH FLY

*Scaptia* sp. >

Horse flies are typically thought of as pests. Members of this group bite people and will return again and again if swatted away. Similar to mosquitoes, only females will bite people as they need a blood-meal to help develop their eggs. Females have a stout, piercing mouthpart that jabs like a large needle when they bite. Male horse flies only feed on flowers and are thought to be important pollinators, especially for Australian native plants. Their larvae are predators, living in semiaquatic habitats like stream edges.

> **Location:** *Species known from all states in Australia.*

**FACT**
One species of horse fly is named after Beyoncé (*Scaptia beyonceae*) and has a golden bum!

These large flies will follow you around until they get their blood-meal.

# ROBBER FLIES

## FAMILY ASILIDAE

### BLUE ROBBER FLY

*Maira* sp.

Robber flies are predators both in their adult and larval stage. They often prey on herbivorous or plant-feeding insects and are thought to play an important role in managing insect populations. They can catch their prey mid-flight! When they mate, like this pair, they can also fly while still attached.

**Location:** *Coastal regions of the Northern Territory and northern Queensland.*

The moustache on a robber fly's face is called a mystax and is composed of stiff, dense bristles. This mystax is thought to protect the fly from its struggling prey.

### COMMON GOLDEN ROBBER FLY

*Zosteria rubens*

Robber flies often wait to ambush their prey. They can be seen resting on tree trunks or leaves like this individual before they spot prey and quickly fly off to ambush it.

**Location:** *Southeast Queensland and northern New South Wales.*

# SOLDIER FLIES

## FAMILY STRATIOMYIDAE

### BLACK SOLDIER FLY

*Hermetia illucens*

If you have a compost heap, you will know this fly well. Black soldier fly maggots efficiently breakdown food scraps and garden clippings. Nothing special is required to attract these little nutrient recyclers. As long as there is a compost heap, the adult flies will find it and lay their eggs in it. The maggots remain buried in the compost until they are ready to pupate and crawl to a dry area.

**Location:** *Found in every state of Australia, particularly urban areas.*

# SIGNAL FLIES

## FAMILY PLATYSTOMATIDAE

### STALK-EYED SIGNAL FLY

*Achias australis*

**Photograph:** John Lenagan.

Males of this group have their eyes placed at the end of long stalks and look like the hammerhead sharks of the fly world. They use these wide eyes to fight each other and can compare their stalk-length to determine if they want to fight or not. This fighting is over access to females and food resources like rotting fruit and even mammalian dung. While these may not seem like worthy reasons to fight, these flies need these resources to reproduce and are therefore key to their continuation.

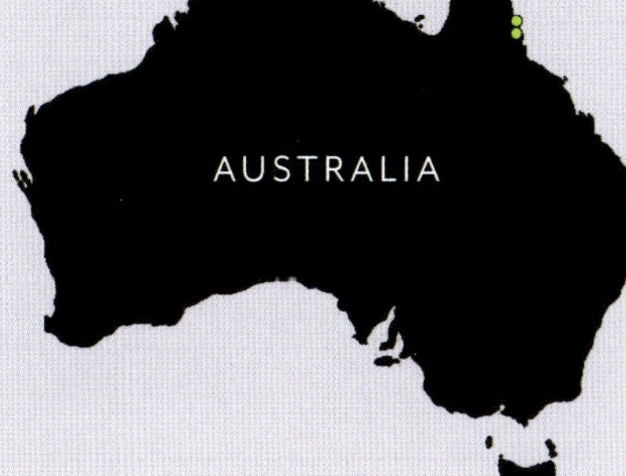


**Location:** *Northern Queensland.*

CHAPTER 5

# BUTTERFLIES AND MOTHS

## ORDER LEPIDOPTERA

The small green-banded blue butterfly has cannibalistic caterpillars.

# INTRODUCTION

Butterflies and moths make up the Order Lepidoptera and are a diverse group both in their colours and ecology. The larvae of butterflies and moths are called caterpillars, and they can feed on a wide variety of plants. Some caterpillars live for as little as a couple of weeks while other species can live for a few years. There is no clear or single difference between butterflies and moths. Instead, there are a set of families which are called butterflies and another set that we call moths. There are a few traits that can help you tell the difference between a butterfly and a moth.

Butterflies and moths have a long, tubular mouthpart called a proboscis. This lets them drink from flowers and access nectar that other animals cannot. They keep this long tube curled up until they need to use it.

## BUTTERFLIES

Cairns birdwing (*Ornithoptera euphorion*) male

- Active during the day.
- Typically colourful.
- Often have clubbed-antennae.
- Rests with wings folded up.
- Pupates as a chrysalis.

## MOTHS

White-brow hawk moth (*Gnathothlibus eras*)

- Usually active at night.
- Typically dull-coloured.
- Often have feathery or straight antennae.
- Rests with wings folded down by sides.
- Larva makes a shelter or cocoon to pupate.

## FACT

Butterflies gather minerals from river-edges, dead animals, and even sweat! Male butterflies need these minerals to prepare a package of food and sperm, called a nuptial gift that they give to females.

Like a moth to a flame: moths have evolved to use the moon and stars to navigate, a process called transverse orientation. Our artificial lights overwhelm these uniquely adapted senses, and they can be attracted to our artificial lights.

# BUTTERFLIES

## SWALLOWTAIL BUTTERFLIES

FAMILY PAPILIONIDAE

### RICHMOND BIRDWING BUTTERFLY

*Ornithoptera richmondia* >

The Richmond birdwing butterfly is the smallest birdwing butterfly found in Australia. It was once common in Queensland and northern New South Wales, but loss of rainforest habitat and the introduction of an invasive vine, the Dutchman's pipe (*Aristolochia littoralis*), have made it rare. Its caterpillars feed on a native vine called the birdwing butterfly vines (*Pararistolochia praevenosa* and *P. laheyana*), which are related to the invasive Dutchman's pipe. Both vines are toxic, but the caterpillar can use the toxins from the native vine to make themselves toxic.

This species is listed as vulnerable to extinction in Queensland.

**You can help this vulnerable butterfly by planting its host plant.**

> ***Location:*** *Southeast Queensland and northern New South Wales.*

### CAIRNS BIRDWING BUTTERFLY

*Ornithoptera euphorion* ^

The Cairns birdwing is a common sight in the tropical rainforests of northern Queensland. As soon as a female emerges from her chrysalis, a male butterfly will try to find her and dazzle her with his vivid green. Male butterflies 'dance' by flying over the female, flapping their vibrant green wings, and dusting the female with pheromones. If the female is impressed by this dance, she may let him mate with her. Several males can be seen chasing after female butterflies or each other, all in the attempt to secure a mate.

> ***Location:*** *Tropical regions of northern Queensland.*

**At rest, the caterpillar looks like poop.**

**When disturbed, it will inflate its osmeterium.**

### ORCHARD SWALLOWTAIL BUTTERFLY

*Papilio aegeus* >

Imagine that your goal in life is to look like a poo. Well, that is the strategy this orchard swallowtail caterpillar has, and it works well! These caterpillars can feed and rest on the top of leaves, camouflaged as bird droppings. If their poo-disguise fails and they are disturbed, the caterpillar can inflate its pink osmeterium, an appendage on their head that resembles a snake's tongue and has a strong scent. All swallowtail caterpillars have this adaptation and it helps scare off predators.

^ ***Location:*** *Throughout Queensland, New South Wales, Victoria and some regions of the Northern Territory.*

## ULYSSES BUTTERFLY

*Papilio ulysses* >

This blue jewel of tropical Queensland can be vibrant one minute and invisible the next. While at rest, the Ulysses butterfly keeps its wings closed, exposing the brown underside of its wings. This underside helps it blend in with its environment, but when disturbed, the butterfly takes flight, exposing a flash of blue on the top of its wings. This is thought to startle predators, allowing the butterfly to escape. Both males and females are metallic blue, but females have extra metallic blue crescents on their hindwings.

Female

Brown underside of wing

> ***Location:*** *Tropical regions of Queensland.*

Males are known to be attracted to any blue object. These blue colours may resemble a female butterfly or another male encroaching on their territory.

## BLUE TRIANGLE BUTTERFLY

*Graphium choredon* <

These butterflies can be seen flying rapidly from flower to flower as they feed. They will also chase each other, as they can be territorial. The species is common in remnant rainforests and dry monsoon forests but can also be seen in suburban areas where their host plants grow. Male blue triangle butterflies will 'dance' or fly rapidly over the female as she sits and waits. The wings of these butterflies are semi-transparent, allowing light to illuminate their blue colours more vibrantly. These colours and the pheromones from the male can 'dazzle' the female so that she mates.

> ***Location:*** *Coastal regions of Queensland and New South Wales.*

## CLEARWING SWALLOWTAIL OR BIG GREASY BUTTERFLY

*Cressida cressida* >

While all butterflies and moths have some scales covering their wings, the clearwing butterfly has very few. This makes their wings almost transparent. The role of this clear wing is unknown, as these butterflies do not require camouflage from predators. Their caterpillars feed on poisonous vines (*Aristolochia* spp.) and the bold red and black colours on the male help advertise this toxicity while the female has few markings. Males of this species are also uniquely larger than the females. This is thought to be a result of mate competition, as males defend an area of host plants, chasing off other males and searching for a female to mate with.

> ***Location:*** *Northern regions of Western Australia, the Northern Territory, and New South Wales, but throughout much of Queensland.*

Males are more colourful and uniquely larger than females.

# NYMPH BUTTERFLIES

## FAMILY NYMPHALIDAE

### MONARCH OR WANDERER BUTTERFLY

*Danaus plexippus* >

The monarch butterfly is native to North America, but it is now commonly seen in Australia too, where it has become naturalised as an exotic species. How is this different from an invasive species? The monarch caterpillars only feed on milkweed (*Asclepias* spp.) and cotton bush (*Gomphocarpuis fruticosus*) and are not thought to compete with our native butterflies. Because of this, the monarch butterfly is not considered an invasive pest, and is instead called exotic. The weeds that monarch caterpillars eat have toxic properties as well and the adult butterflies can use it. The striking orange and black colours on these butterflies warn predators of this toxicity.

This caterpillar is getting ready to moult into a chrysalis (pupa).

This butterfly has been in Australia since the 1860s.

> ***Location:*** *Found throughout Australia.*

**These butterflies migrate** over 4,000kms in their native range of North America, but they do not migrate in Australia. Instead, these butterflies breed year-round in the warmer temperatures of Queensland, while in Sydney they can be seen resting in large groups in trees. So many butterflies can rest on one branch, that it can droop!

### BLUE TIGER BUTTERFLY

*Tirumala hamata* ^

During the long, dry season these butterflies can be found sheltering together in large numbers. They most commonly do this along the coast, and some years can see large enough numbers of this species that it may appear as though it is raining butterflies. They reproduce during the wet season or summer when there is plenty of new growth on their host plants for their caterpillars to feed on.

> ***Location:*** *Queensland, New South Wales, Western Australia and the Northern Territory.*

### COMMON CROW BUTTERFLY

*Euploea corinna* v

The common crow can live in a wide range of habitats since their caterpillars feed on many different plants, including many that are toxic. Their caterpillars are bright orange, advertising this toxicity. They also have a golden, metallic chrysalis which looks like someone's lost jewellery in the bush. Large numbers of these butterflies can be seen in the dry season when they migrate further inland and shelter together. In the wet season, these butterflies can also migrate further south to New South Wales, Victoria, and some parts of South Australia.

> ***Location:*** *Western Australia, the Northern Territory, Queensland and some parts of New South Wales.*

# BLUES AND SWIFTS

## FAMILY LYCAENIDAE

### SMALL GREEN-BANDED BLUE BUTTERFLY

*Psychonotis caelius* <

This species begins life as a small, green caterpillar that hides on underside of ash tree leaves (*Alphitonia* spp.). However, the caterpillars of this species do not get along well with each other and are known to be cannibalistic! If they make it to adulthood, they become vibrant blue butterflies. While some blue can be seen on this resting butterfly, the top side of its wings is very bright, so when it takes off, it flashes bright blue.

> ***Location:*** *Coastal regions of Queensland and New South Wales.*

### CYCAD BLUE BUTTERFLY

*Theclinesthes onycha* ^

You can find several of these butterflies flitting around the new fronds of cycads. This species lays its eggs on the young plant tissue, where their caterpillars later feed. If too many eggs are laid, the new fronds of the cycad can be destroyed. This species' ability to feed on cycads is impressive considering the toxicity of these plants. The butterflies feed on native cycads, but also ornamental species from other countries, making some gardeners consider the butterfly a pest.

> ***Location:*** *Coastal regions of Queensland and New South Wales.*

### THE MOTH BUTTERFLY

*Liphyra brassolis* >

This butterfly lays its eggs near the large, leafy nests of weaver ants. The caterpillars that hatch out look like a freshly baked pie because they have a thick covering over their body called a carapace. These caterpillars then enter the ants' nest and search for ant larvae. The ants try to attack the invader, but the thick carapace protects it. Once the caterpillar finds ant larvae, it lifts its hard carapace and drags an ant larva underneath. It reseals its carapace to the surface of the leaves and eats the ant larva! These caterpillars later pupate inside of the weaver ants' nest within their hard carapace. The adult that emerges is covered in scales that protect it from the ants and allow it to escape the nest. This butterfly is drably coloured and active around dusk, making it seem more like a moth.

> ***Location:*** *Northern regions of Western Australia, the Northern Territory and Queensland.*

**FACT**

**The caterpillars of this butterfly are carnivorous!**

**Photograph by:** Dr. Peter Samson.

# MOTHS

## EMPEROR MOTHS

FAMILY SATURNIIDAE

**These moths are also called silk moths, but the silk used in clothing is produced by another group, the silkworms (Family Bombycidae). Both groups of moths use silk to form a cocoon within which they pupate.**

### VARIABLE EMPEROR MOTH

*Syntherata melvilla* <

This moth can vary in colour from bright yellow to dark red, but no one knows why they vary. One hypothesis is that their colour is related to the plant that they feed on. The different colours may help them blend in with bark if they are red or dead leaves if they are yellow. This species' caterpillars can feed on several plants including a few species of mangroves.

> ***Location:** Northern regions of Western Australia and the Northern Territory.*

### HERCULES MOTH

*Coscinocera hercules* ^

This enormous moth can have a wingspan of 27cm, but the adults do not live for long! This is because adults have no mouthparts and instead of feeding they live on fats gained from their caterpillar stage. The caterpillars feed on several rainforest plants, but most commonly can be found on the bleeding-heart tree (*Homalanthus nutans*). Over three months, the caterpillars grow to about the size of a hotdog and can weigh up to 29g.

> ***Location:** Rainforests of New Guinea and northern Queensland.*

### HELENA GUM MOTH

*Opodiphthera helena* v

The caterpillars of this moth can feed on a variety of gum trees (*Eucalyptus* spp.) which may explain why it can be found in so many different parts of Australia. Once they are large enough, the caterpillars spin a silk cocoon on their host tree which hardens. This hard case protects the vulnerable pupa from any potential intruders.

> ***Location:** Through out Australia.*

## SWALLOWTAIL MOTHS

FAMILY URANIIDAE

### ZODIAC MOTH

*Alcides metaurus* >

Not a butterfly, but a brightly-coloured moth! Some moths have not read the book about what they are meant to do. This species flies during the day and is brightly coloured. These colours serve as a warning to predators that it is toxic. They gain their toxicity while they are caterpillars, feeding on the leaves of toxic vines and storing those toxins in their body as they grow.

In warmer months, you can find large numbers of moths when they all come together to breed.

> ***Location:** Northern regions of the Northern Territory and Queensland.*

# SPHYNX OR HAWK MOTHS

## FAMILY SPHINGIDAE

### COPROSMA HAWK MOTH

*Cizara ardeniae* ∨

Can you see someone looking back at you? The golden spots on this species may serve to scare off any potential predators who may think another animal is looking back at them. The green patches and yellow outline can also distort the shape of the moth, making it not look like a moth at all. This species is named after the mirror bush (*Coprosma repens*) that the caterpillars feed on.

> **Location:** *East coast of Australia.*

### WHITE-BROW HAWK MOTH

*Gnathothlibus eras* >

This is one of the largest and most common hawk moths found in Australia. Their caterpillars feed on several plants, including native grapevines. Their caterpillars are also very large and speckled with white eyespots outlined with blue. The adults have vibrant orange hindwings that are visible when they fly. Hawk moths, like this species are important pollinators.

> **Location:** *Northern regions of the Northern Territory and the coasts of Queensland and New South Wales.*

Photograph by: John Lenagan.

### GARDENIA BEE HAWK

*Cephonodes kingii* ∧

When this species first leaves its leaf-litter pupation chamber, it is covered in green scales. Over time, it sheds the scales off of its wings until they are clear. Their abdomens have a bright yellow and black stripe, and this mix of characters makes these moths look like a large bee!

> **Location:** *Northern parts of Western Australia and the Northern Territory, and throughout Queensland, New South Wales and Victoria.*

### AUSTRALIAN HUMMINGBIRD HAWKMOTH

*Macroglossum hirundo* ‹

These caterpillars can vary in colour. These different colours may help them blend in with their surroundings or serve as warning colours. When disturbed, the caterpillar will rear up and produce a bubble of vomit. This smells and likely tastes bad enough to deter a predator.

> **Location:** *Coastal regions of Queensland and New South Wales.*

# BAGWORM MOTHS

## FAMILY PSYCHIDAE

Bagworms or casemoths are most known for the shelter that they drag around as caterpillars. They will construct their home or case from silk and debris from their environment. They can use twigs or leaves for this, but the shelters are typically unique to each species. Once they are ready to pupate, each caterpillar will seal off the entrance to their home and pupate inside their case.

> **Location:** *Throughout Australia.*

# BAG-SHELTER MOTHS

## FAMILY NOTODONTIDAE

### PROCESSIONARY CATERPILLAR

*Ochrogaster lunifer* >

**Photograph:** Dr. Mizuki Uemura.

Processionary caterpillars are covered in defensive hairs called setae that can irritate the skin, so if you see a hairy caterpillar – do not touch it! These caterpillars follow one another in a line as they search for new food or a place to pupate. Scientists study these caterpillars by using marking powder to follow their procession.

> **Location:** *Throughout Australia, except Tasmania*

This caterpillar wears a homemade hat!

# TUFT MOTHS

## FAMILY NOLIDAE

### THE GUM-LEAF SKELETONISER

*Uraba lugens* <

As it grows, the caterpillar of the gum-leaf skeletoniser will stack its old head-capsules on top of one another. Here you can see how much the caterpillar has grown by the stack of old heads, with the smaller heads from younger instars stacked on top, to the larger heads from later instars stacked below.

> ***Location:*** *Eucalypt forests of Western Australia, South Australia, Victoria, Tasmania, New South Wales and Queensland.*

# SLUG AND NOCTUID MOTHS

## FAMILY LIMACODIDAE AND NOCTUIDAE

STINGING SPINES

### SLUG MOTH

*Anaxidia lozogramma* ^

The stinging spines that cover the bodies of slug moth caterpillars are fragile, hollow tubes. If broken off, the venom inside each spine will sting whoever has bothered the caterpillar. The bright colours on these caterpillars help warn of their venomous defence, while the caterpillars often feed on the undersides of leaves to avoid any potential threat.

AUSTRALIA

> ***Location:*** *Coastal Queensland and northern New South Wales.*

Endangered species

**Photograph:** John Bromilow.

### BOGONG MOTH

*Agrotis infusa* ^

In late summer, thousands of bogong moths fly south to mountaintops where they take shelter in cool caves or other crevices. This annual migration is an important food resource to animals like the mountain pygmy-possum. Indigenous Australians would also go to the mountains to harvest these moths. The moths could be knocked down with a stick and pour off the walls like water. The adult moths were then cooked and eaten whole or pounded into cakes.

> ***Location:*** *Western Australia, South Australia, Victoria, Tasmania, New South Wales and Queensland.*

### JOSEPH'S COAT MOTH

*Agarista agricola* ^

The Joseph's coat moth is a day-flying moth, with bright colours that advertise its toxicity. It is equally colourful as a caterpillar with black, white and orange stripes and spoon-like projections. As caterpillars, they feed on several Australian native grapevines. Once they are large enough, the caterpillars chew pieces of bark to form a pupal chamber on a branch. This chamber blends in with the branch and gives them a safe place to pupate until they emerge as an adult.

> ***Location:*** *Widespread in the Northern Territory, Queensland, New South Wales and Victoria.*

# FRUIT-PIERCING AND UNDERWING MOTHS

## FAMILY EREBIDAE

### GRANNY'S CLOAK MOTH

*Speiredonia spectans* ^

This large moth is active at night, taking shelter in caves, hollowed trees, or even our homes during the day. This species can vary in colour, from browns to purples and the eyespots on their wings are thought to deter predators. They can easily be confused with the northern or southern old lady moth, but the granny's cloak moth is usually purple and has a second set of eye spots on their hindwings.

> ***Location:*** *Queensland, Northern Territory, New South Wales, Victoria and Tasmania.*

### PINK UNDERWING MOTH

*Phyllodes imperialis* >

This moth's forewings resemble dead leaves and even have silver markings that look like leaf-mines left by other insects. They fold their wings over their body to disguise themselves as a fallen leaf. If this camouflage fails, they can flash the bright pink spots on their hindwings to startle a predator long enough for the moth to escape.

> ***Location:*** *Coastal regions of Queensland and New South Wales.*

### TROPICAL GYPSY MOTH

*Lymantria pelospila* <

This species feeds on gum leaves (*Eucalyptus* spp.) as a caterpillar. Once it is ready to pupate, it builds a golden silk chamber under the eucalypt bark. If it is a male, the small moth will emerge, expand its wings and fly to the nearest female. If it is a female, it will barely move, waiting on the males to come to them instead since they cannot fly!

> ***Location:*** *Across Australia and Southeast Asia.*

## DID YOU KNOW?

**Several male butterflies and moths can inflate their hair pencils, or coremata, to attract females.**

**Photograph:** Dave Rentz.

### BAPHOMET MOTH

*Creatonotos gangis* <

Males can increase the amount of pheromone they release by having a large surface area to release it from. By blowing up these hair pencils covered in pheromones, the moths can smell very attractive to a female.

> ***Location:*** *Northern regions of Western Australia, the Northern Territory and Queensland.*

**Photograph:** Dianne Clarke.

### CROCKER'S FROTHER

*Amerila crokeri* ^

When disturbed, this moth can blow out bubbles of yellow liquid on its thorax! As the liquid comes out, it also makes a sizzling noise as though the liquid is a horrible acid. These defence bubbles are like frothed milk, giving the species its common name.

> ***Location:*** *Northern regions of Western Australia, the Northern Territory, and coastal regions of Queensland and New South Wales.*

# INCHWORMS OR LOOPERS

## FAMILY GEOMETRIDAE

**This family of moths** is named after their caterpillars, which inch across the ground. The family name, Geometridae means 'to measure the Earth' and the way that their caterpillars walk resembles someone trying to measure a distance, step by step. Adult moths are often well camouflaged and their broad, outstretched wings blend in seamlessly with their background.

### ACACIA POLLEN MOTH

*Traminda rubra* ^

The caterpillars of this moth blend in with wattle flowers (*Acacia* spp.). This cleverly disguised caterpillar can safely feed on the pollen of the flowers until it is ready to pupate between the wattle leaves, where it suspends itself on silk. The adult moths are brown to blend in with tree bark.

> ***Location:*** *Coastal regions of Queensland.*

Can you spot this caterpillar's head and legs?

### GUMTREE BIZARRE LOOPER MOTH

*Eucyclodes metaspila* ^

The gumtree bizarre looper moth begins its life hiding in plain sight. Its caterpillar looks like a dead leaf and feeds on gum leaves (*Eucalyptus* spp.). This species is a bit of a shapeshifter and will curl up to disguise itself when it rests or is disturbed. Once it grows large enough, it will pupate into a small green moth, which can be just as hidden in plain sight on green leaves!

> ***Location:*** *The Northern Territory, Queensland and New South Wales.*

### 4 O'CLOCK MOTH

*Dysphania numana* >

The caterpillars of this moth are bright yellow with black spots. When they are not feeding, they can be seen resting near the ends of branches with their body extended. By doing this, they disguise themselves as flower stems instead. When they pupate, they do not spin a cocoon, but simply fold a leaf together. The adult moths have unique purple or dark blue wings and can be seen flying late in the afternoon or around 4 O'Clock!

> ***Location:*** *Northern regions of Western Australia, the Northern Territory and Queensland.*

### BEAUTIFUL LEAF MOTH

*Gastrophora henricaria* >

The caterpillars of this moth resemble the ends of branches and will rest in a still, extended pose. They feed on gum leaves (*Eucalyptus* spp.) and can be found throughout much of the southeast sections of Australia. Adults are well-camouflaged as well, with light brown wings both from above and below. Their brown forewings hide their bright orange hindwings until they are ready for a display.

∨ ***Location:*** *Queensland, New South Wales, the ACT, Victoria and South Australia.*

# WOOD MOTHS

## FAMILY COSSIDAE

Photograph: Ethan Beaver.

**The caterpillars of wood moths have been harvested by Indigenous Australians for thousands of years. To harvest the caterpillars, Australia's First Peoples had to study the moths' lifecycles and which plants the moths used. In many ways, Indigenous Australians are the first scientists.**

### GIANT WOOD MOTH

*Endoxyla cinereus* >

This moth takes two to three years to complete its life cycle! The caterpillar bores into the trunk or branch of a eucalypt tree, making a large chamber inside. Here, it spends years feeding on the callus tissue just under the bark. When it is ready to pupate, the caterpillar will chew a large hole and clear its smaller initial entrance hole. It then backs into the tree to pupate. You can find these large holes in gum trees in summer, sometimes with a pupal case sticking out once the moth has emerged. The adults have no mouths and only live for a few days! The caterpillars are very nutritious and eaten by Indigenous Australians.

HEAVIEST MOTH IN THE WORLD!

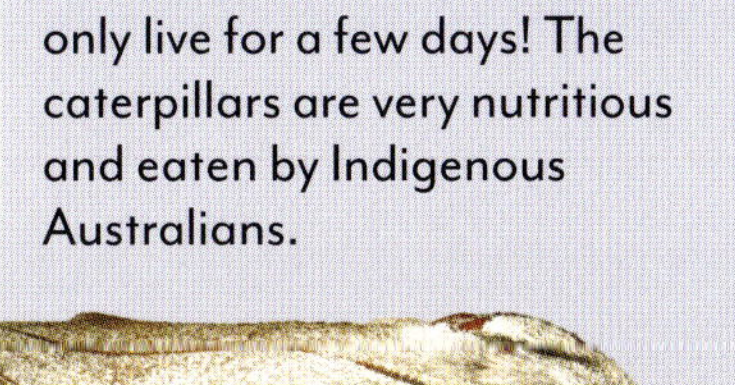

> ***Location:*** *Queensland, New South Wales, Victoria, South Australia and Western Australia.*

### THE WITCHETTY GRUB MOTH

*Endoxyla leucomochla* ^

The caterpillars of this moth are thought to be the original witchetty grubs. This name comes from the Arabana people of Central Australia, who harvest caterpillars that they call, 'mako witjuti.' Mako means 'grub,' while witjuti is a wattle shrub (*Acacia kempeana*). This species' caterpillars feed on the roots of wattle shrubs. When the caterpillars come closer to the soil surface to pupate, they are more easily gathered. This time is celebrated by many Indigenous Australians with songs and dances.

AUSTRALIA

> ***Location:*** *Western Australia, Central Australia, South Australia, Victoria and New South Wales.*

# GHOST MOTHS

## FAMILY HEPIALIDAE

### GHOST MOTHS

*Aenetus eximia* >

This species begins its life feeding in leaf litter, but later bores into the trunk of a tree. The caterpillar excavates a tunnel inside the tree that travels straight down. It hides in here, and feeds near the bark of the tree under a covering made of silk and sawdust. Their lifecycle is thought to take several years, with adults only emerging after heavy rain or other weather events.

> ***Location:*** *Rainforests of southeast Queensland, New South Wales and Victoria.*

Photograph: Ethan Beaver.

**Ghost moths often vary in colour. This species can be lime green or pale blue!**

CHAPTER 6

# TRUE BUGS

## ORDER HEMIPTERA

This eucalyptus tip-wilter bug can blend in with bark, while its nymphs are so colourful they are often called clown bugs!

While true bugs can look very different, they typically have a similar, long straw-like mouthpart called a rostrum. Most species use this mouth to pierce plant tissue and suck up plant fluids. However, there are some predatory species that can use this piercing mouth to stab prey.

**FACT**
**Flat-headed leafhoppers are flat enough to hide under bark.**

# INTRODUCTION

True bugs are members of the Order Hemiptera. The word 'bug' was first used to refer to any insect in this order, whether it was a cicada, an assassin bug, or a stink bug. Since then, the word has been generalised to refer to several different types of invertebrates. The groups in this chapter are called true bugs because they are the original bugs.

All bugs are hemimetabolous, meaning they lay eggs, that hatch into nymphs who eventually moult into adult bugs. Nymphs look like smaller versions of their adult forms but lack wings and cannot reproduce. Most adults can be identified based on the presence of wings. Here, you can see a black prince cicada (*Psaltoda sp.*) moulting from its last nymphal instar (phase) into an adult, winged cicada.

Bugs typically have a rostrum alongside two antennae and compound eyes. They can also have ocelli or simple eyes on the top of their head. The ocelli can sense light vs dark or detect movement. Bugs also have a scutellum or triangle-shaped plate that usually extends from their thorax over their abdomen. The scutellum is uniquely shaped across the different groups of bugs, with shield bugs having their entire back covered by their scutellum, almost like a beetle's elytra. Most bugs also have two pairs of wings, with some having thickened forewings, as seen in this gum stink bug (*Poecilometis gravis*), while others can have clear wings like this thin-striped wattle cicada (*Ewartia roberti*).

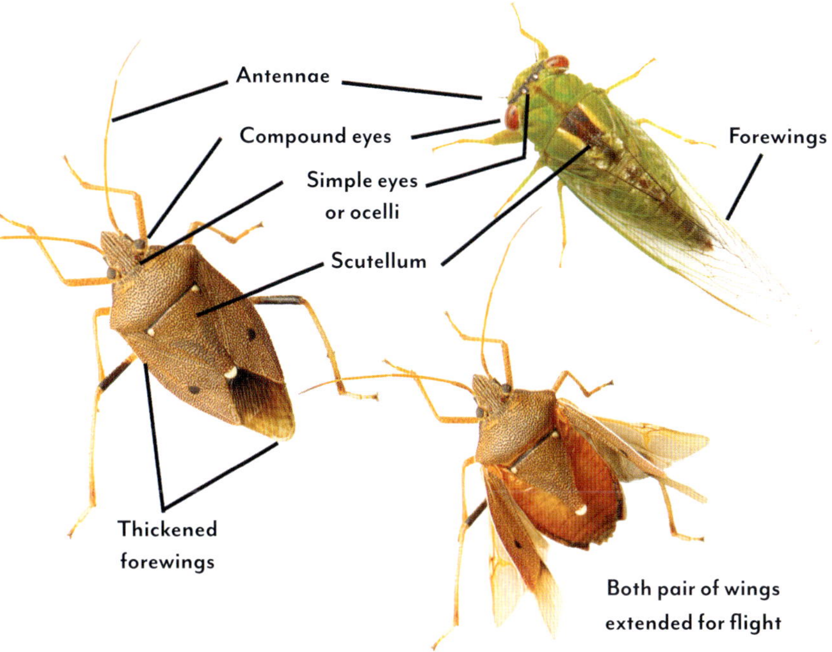

# ASSASSIN BUGS

## FAMILY REDUVIIDAE

### COMMON ASSASSIN BUG

*Pristhesancus plagipennis* >

Assassin bugs hide themselves amongst the leaves or flowers, waiting for their prey to come to them. It will catch its prey by stabbing it swiftly with its long rostrum. The bug will then inject its prey with a digestive enzyme that liquifies the prey's insides. The assassin bug can then slurp up this delicious smoothie, leaving the exoskeleton of their prey behind. This bug is also known as the bee killer as it often hunts at flowers where the European honey bee (*Apis mellifera*) visits. This bee has been introduced to Australia to pollinate our crops and give us honey.

> ***Location:*** *Throughout much of Queensland and New South Wales.*

**FACT**

**Assassin bugs have a painful bite! The same digestive enzyme that they use on their prey can be used on us to cause intense pain.**

**Assassin bugs turn their prey into a partially digested smoothie!**

**Orange and black colours like those seen on this bug can warn predators that this insect bites back!**

### ORANGE ASSASSIN BUG

*Gminatus* spp. <

These orange assassin bugs have been seen hunting in small groups, while most assassin bugs are entirely solitary. These groups are likely to be potential mates gathering to hunt in areas with abundant prey. An easy target for these bugs are the entrances to stingless bee hives. Here, the predatory bug can capture a worker bee on its way back to the nest. Like other assassin bugs, this species is brightly coloured to warn of its painful bite, but it is also more vibrant than most as it is almost entirely orange. If they need to escape a threat or search for more food, this species can also fly.

> ***Location:*** *Found in every state, but more common in southern regions of Australia.*

### RED TIGER ASSASSIN BUG

*Havinthus rufovarius* >

This red and black assassin hides under the bark of gum trees. It will lay in wait for the many other insects which take shelter under this bark, then jab them with its long rostrum. If it is exposed or disturbed, it can quickly fly away to another tree to escape danger. The bright red on this species warns of its painful bite, but these colours can vary between individuals. Some may look almost entirely black, and blend in well with burned trees, while others have more red.

> ***Location:*** *Found in every state except Tasmania.*

# CICADAS

## SUPERFAMILY CICADOIDEA

Some species of cicadas call in the middle of the day when it is the hottest. This is when most predators are seeking shelter from the heat, so the cicadas can call and have less risk of being found then eaten.

### BLACK TREE-TICKER

*Birrima varians* >

Cicadas are best known for their loud calls. For most species, only males call and they sing, or more appropriately scream, to attract a female. Cicadas call using their tymbal organs, which are ribbed membranes just under their wings. Muscles attached to the tymbals cause the ribs of the membrane to buckle and when they do, it makes a sound called a pulse. These pulses are made rapidly and will make up each cicada's call. A tensor muscle can then make the membrane of the tymbal more rigid to increase the volume of the sound. Both males and females need to hear these calls though, and they do so with a pair of tympana on the underside of their abdomens. It is hard to see these tympana as they are each covered by a large, plate-like structure called an operculum. These cicada 'ears' are mainly tuned to the frequency of their own calls.

> ***Location:*** *Patchy distribution in Queensland and northern New South Wales.*

### TIGER CHERRYNOSE

*Macrotristria godingi* ^

The tiger cherrynose is named after the dark red spot on its face which resembles a nose. This is not the cicada's true nose though, as they smell using their small antennae. This species is common in summer around the dry regions of northern Queensland. They feed on the roots of gum trees (*Eucalyptus spp.*) as nymphs, then emerge in late November to sing and breed. Species in this genus are known for their loud, whining call which sounds like, "EEEEEEEERRH."

> ***Location:*** *Northern Queensland.*

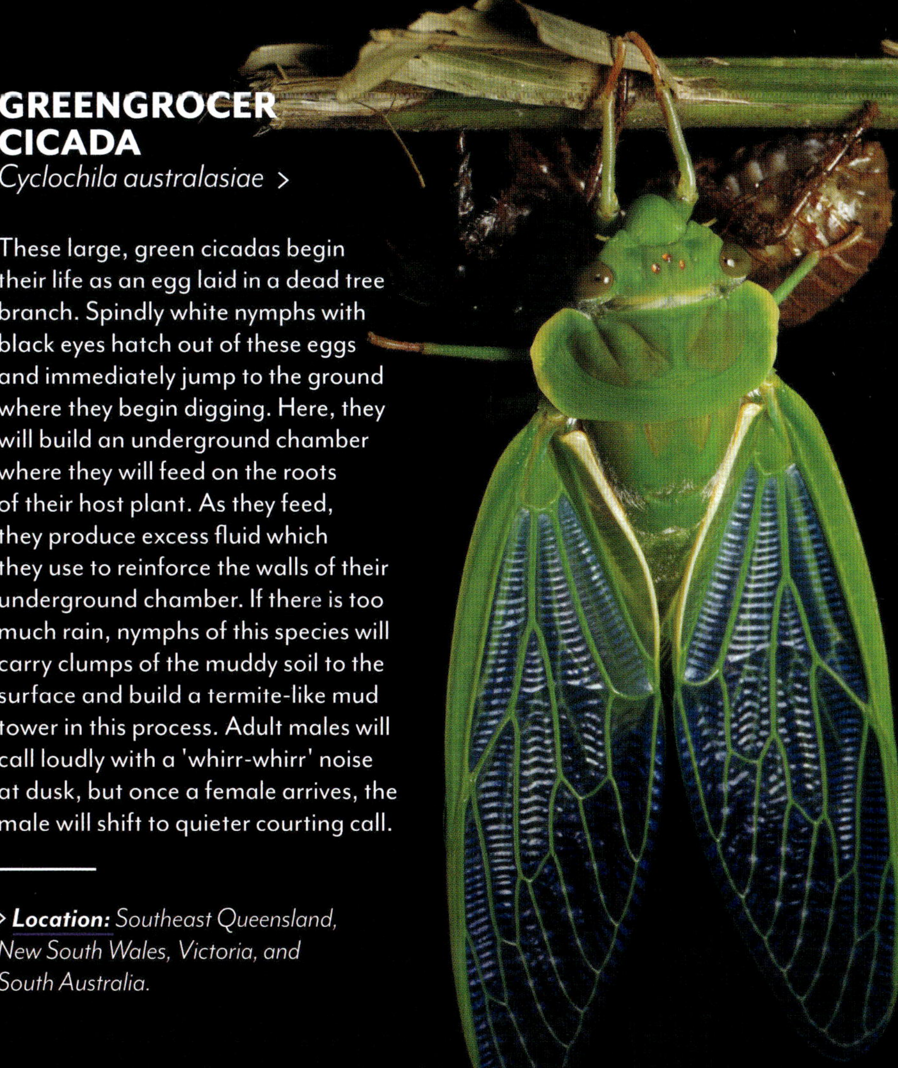

### GREENGROCER CICADA

*Cyclochila australasiae* >

These large, green cicadas begin their life as an egg laid in a dead tree branch. Spindly white nymphs with black eyes hatch out of these eggs and immediately jump to the ground where they begin digging. Here, they will build an underground chamber where they will feed on the roots of their host plant. As they feed, they produce excess fluid which they use to reinforce the walls of their underground chamber. If there is too much rain, nymphs of this species will carry clumps of the muddy soil to the surface and build a termite-like mud tower in this process. Adult males will call loudly with a 'whirr-whirr' noise at dusk, but once a female arrives, the male will shift to quieter courting call.

> ***Location:*** *Southeast Queensland, New South Wales, Victoria, and South Australia.*

Female bladder cicada

**FACT**
Males of this species are mostly empty inside with a large, hollow abdomen. Females lack this.

## BLADDER CICADA
*Cystosoma saundersii* ^

Sounds produced by the cicada's tymbals are amplified in their abdomen and many males will expand their abdomen before they start to call. This species has taken this expansion to the extreme with a large, hollow abdomen. It is also named after this large abdomen, which resembles a full bladder. As they call, the sound resonates in the hollow chamber of their body, giving this species a rattle-sounding call. Males usually call around dusk and continue until it becomes completely dark. They can be found in several gardens or on the edges of rainforest, but this species is also hard to spot as males often call from the tops of trees, and the species looks like a green leaf.

> **Location:** *Patchy distribution through Queensland and New South Wales.*

## SMALL BOTTLE CICADA
*Glaucopsaltria viridis* ∨

The small bottle cicada has the same strategy as the bladder cicada for amplifying its call. Males have enormous, hollow abdomens and their call sounds like an endless whistle or a boiling kettle. They sing in rainforests and along creeks just after dusk. Thunderstorms can also set their chorus off. But cicadas do not begin their life so loudly. Their large nymphs usually emerge from the ground in the early hours before or after sunset. Once they crawl onto the trunk of a tree or any nearby vertical surface, they will moult into their adult form. This process can take hours and involves inflating their wings with their haemolymph or watery insect blood. They pump this fluid into their wings to expand them before the fluid is pumped back into their body. Once their wings are dried, they will crawl up the tree and leave their shed skin behind.

> **Location:** *Queensland and northern New South Wales.*

# FLAT BUGS FAMILY ARADIDAE

**FACT**
This flat bug is usually found in large families! Where you spot one, you may find many.

## IRONBARK FLAT BUG
*Drakiessa hackeri* <

Ironbark flat bugs are small, but heavily armoured insects. They live happily under the bark of rotting trees, feeding on the fungi that breaks down wood. They feed using a long, coiled mouthpart that is strange for any bug. This species never grows wings, but it does not need them as it can live on a single log for several generations. Since they rarely move, you can sometimes find these flat bugs in colonies with several adults and nymphs. Flat bugs are usually very dirty, but dirt is good for an aradid! They encrust themselves with soil, hiding their intricately sculptured bodies and making them blend in with their environment.

> **Location:** *Southeast Queensland and northern New South Wales.*

**Photograph:** Dr. Andrew Maynard

# PLANTHOPPERS

## SUPERFAMILY FULGOROIDEA

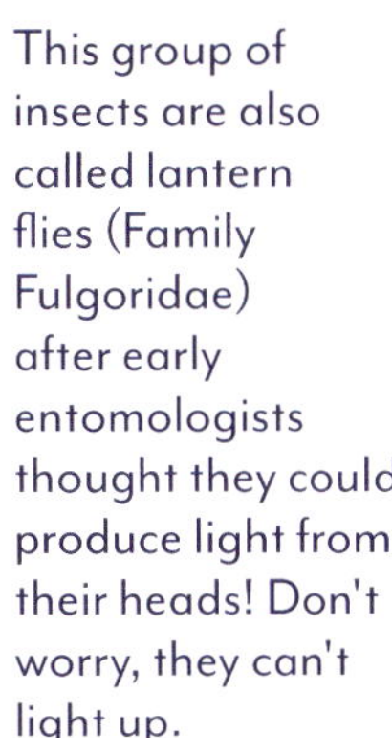

This group of insects are also called lantern flies (Family Fulgoridae) after early entomologists thought they could produce light from their heads! Don't worry, they can't light up.

### GREEN AND BLACK PLANTHOPPER

*Desudaba psittacus* ^

This darkly cloaked insect has secrets under its wings. Like many planthoppers, they can be found walking along the trunks of trees. Their first strategy when they may be under threat is to walk sideways, away from the danger. If this fails, they may open their wings and flash a patch of red. This species also has a bright green abdomen. Aside from making it look like an alien, this abdomen may also be a part of its flash display of colours. When this insect needs to escape, a bright display of colours may confuse the predator shortly enough for the insect to jump away. Like many bugs, they use their rostrum to 'plug in' and feed on plant fluids, but this species pierces through tree bark!

> **Location:** *Coastal regions of southeast Queensland and New South Wales.*

### GREEN-FACED GUM HOPPERS

*Platybrachys decemmacula* ^

Like the other tricky planthoppers, these gum hoppers trick predators about where their head is. You can find adults walking backwards on the trunks of gum trees, making the eyespots on the tips of their wings look like their head. This species has unique eyespots that resemble the multiple eyes of a spider and this may scare off other invertebrates. Nymphs of this planthopper can sometimes have a passenger. These passengers are ectoparasitic, or external parasitic, caterpillars that look like a small backpack. The caterpillar will stay attached to the bug nymph until it is ready to pupate. From here, a small moth called the planthopper parasite moth (*Heteropsyche* sp.) will emerge. These moths lay their eggs on plants and when the eggs hatch, the young caterpillars look for a planthopper host to attach to. Without these bugs, these moths would not exist!

> **Location:** *Queensland, New South Wales, Victoria, South Australia, and Western Australia.*

### PALM PLANTHOPPER

*Magia subocellata* >

The palm planthopper spends its time roaming the trunks of palm trees. They have vibrant blue heads, but their clear wings are tipped with eye spots. This is emphasised by two white spots on their abdomen. These unique patterns can trick a predator about where the planthopper's head is. Knowing where your prey's head is important if you are a predator since this is where you may strike. If these eye spots are struck, the palm planthopper can still escape, although they may have torn wings.

> **Location:** *Coastal regions of Queensland and New South Wales.*

THEY CAN WALK BACKWARDS

# SCALE INSECTS

## SUPERFAMILY COCCOIDEA

### BIRD-OF-PARADISE FLY

*Callipappus* spp. ^

You would never imagine the mate for this lovely, pink winged insect. The insect pictured here is a male scale insect. It is neither a bird, nor a fly. It has four wings, but the hind pair are reduced to small stumps, leaving them with only two functional wings like flies. These males will fly out to a large, blob-like female. Multiple males may land on this female, which is one of the largest scale insects in Australia. Females crawl up trees or posts to beckon to males that they are ready to mate. After mating, females will invert their body to create a type of pouch called a marsupium. The females lay their eggs in this pouch and die shortly after.

> ***Location:*** *Throughout Australia.*

### WATTLE TICK SCALE

*Cryptes baccatus* >

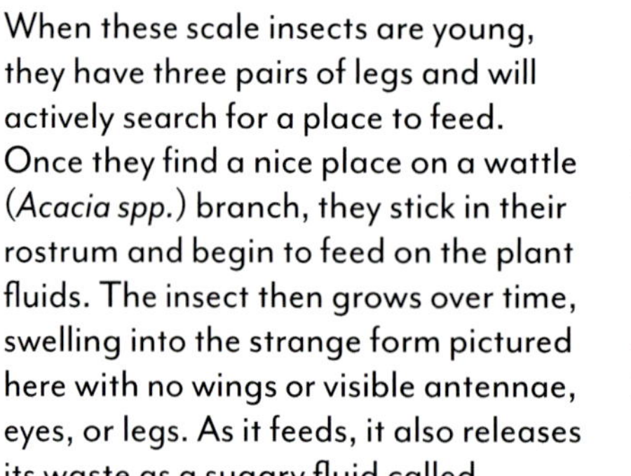

Believe it or not, these white bumps are scale insects.

When these scale insects are young, they have three pairs of legs and will actively search for a place to feed. Once they find a nice place on a wattle (*Acacia spp.*) branch, they stick in their rostrum and begin to feed on the plant fluids. The insect then grows over time, swelling into the strange form pictured here with no wings or visible antennae, eyes, or legs. As it feeds, it also releases its waste as a sugary fluid called honeydew which ants like to feed on. In exchange for the sugary snack, the ants give the scale insects protection from predators. This is especially useful for the scale insect, which has become immobile and unable to escape from any predators.

> ***Location:*** *Queensland, New South Wales, Victoria, South Australia, and Western Australia.*

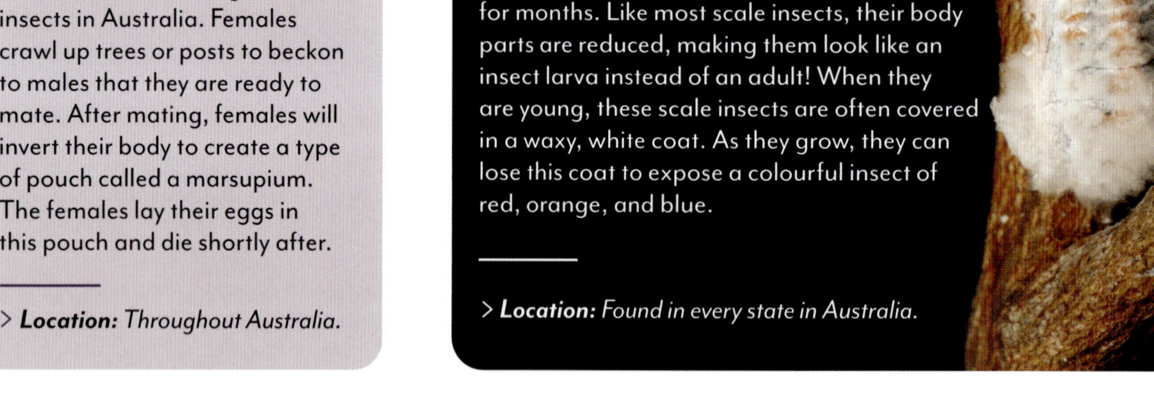

### GIANT RED SCALE INSECT

*Monophlebulus* spp.

These giant red scale insects can crawl slowly over plants until they find the right place to 'plug in' with their rostrum and feed. Once they find a suitable spot, they can stay here for months. Like most scale insects, their body parts are reduced, making them look like an insect larva instead of an adult! When they are young, these scale insects are often covered in a waxy, white coat. As they grow, they can lose this coat to expose a colourful insect of red, orange, and blue.

> ***Location:*** *Found in every state in Australia.*

### GUM GALL SCALE INSECT

*Apiomorpha* spp. <

Scale insects have co-occurred with plants for millions of years, and one of their most interesting adaptations is the formation of galls. When plants have an abnormal growth, that growth is called a gall. These can be caused by several things, including scale insects! While it is not well understood, we do know that scale insects must alter the gene expression of the plant cells around them. This can cause abnormal growths like a nice, large chamber that the scale insect lives and feeds in. Here, you can see the gall that was made by the gum tree and shaped by the scale insect. Inside is a large, female covered with powdery white wax.

> ***Location:*** *Throughout Australia.*

# LEAF-FOOTED BUGS

## FAMILY COREIDAE

### EUCALYPTUS TIP-WILTER

*Amorbus alternatus* >

Look carefully through the new leaves of a eucalyptus tree and you may find the colourful nymphs of this species. The nymphs are yellow and blue, with unique patterns warning that they are not a tasty snack. They feed on the new growth of trees and will cause the tips to wilt in the process. Adults are brown with yellow stripes around their wings. They blend in well with the bark of trees with these less conspicuous colours. In their adult form, they often need to move more to find a mate and to find a good place to lay their eggs.

> ***Location:*** *Throughout southeast Queensland, New South Wales, Victoria, and parts of South Australia.*

# MIRIDS

## FAMILY MIRIDAE

### SUNDEW BUG

*Setocoris* sp. ∨

In the boggy swamps where few things can grow are two carnivorous creatures. The first is a carnivorous plant called a sundew (*Drosera spp.*). These plants can grow in nutrient-poor soils because they capture the nutrients that they need by trapping and digesting insects on their sticky leaves. One insect does not get stuck and is our second carnivore: the sundew bug.

> ***Location:*** *Every state except the Northern Territory.*

# LACE BUG

## FAMILY TINGIDAE

**FACT**

**Lace bugs feed on plant fluids and some species can complete their entire life on one plant!**

The back of these bugs, made up by their pronotum (shoulders) and forewings, is intricately divided into many small windows. This lace-like pattern gives this group their common name, but it also works like an invisibility cloak. Their heads are usually hidden underneath their pronotum while the rest of the lace pattern distorts the bug's body, making them practically invisible on the leaf.

> ***Location:*** *Throughout Australia.*

You will need a magnifying glass to find this alien among moss! These bugs are only 2mm long.

**Photograph:** Dr. Andrew Maynard.

# MOSS BUG

## FAMILY PELORIDIIDAE

### HACKER'S MOSS BUG

*Hackeriella veitchi* <

Deep in the misty mountains, tucked amongst a carpet of lush, green moss is a special and rare bug. Moss looks like a forest compared to the bug who feeds on and completes its lifecycle on this mat of moss. The unique habitat that these bugs prefer can only be found in wet, cool places like mountaintops where plenty of moss grows. Several species can be found across Queensland, Victoria and Tasmania. These unique creatures are coming under threat with climate change though, as their habitats may eventually dry out or burn.

> ***Location:*** *Mountains along the border between Queensland and New South Wales.*

# SHIELD BUGS

## FAMILY SCUTELLERIDAE

### GREEN JEWEL BUG

*Lampromicra senator* >

These little jewels are often mistaken for beetles. This is because their scutellum has been extended across their abdomen and looks like the hardened elytra of a beetle. When it gets too dry or cold, these bugs will gather in groups on the undersides of leaves. They do not feed during this time, but simply huddle together. Sticking together in the jewel bug world is thought to help each bug reduce its chances of being eaten.

AUSTRALIA

> ***Location:*** *Parts of Western Australia, the Northern Territory, Queensland and New South Wales.*

Like all true bugs, this species has a piercing mouthpart under their head called a rostrum instead of the chewing jaws found on beetles.

### HIBISCUS HARLEQUIN BUG

*Tectocoris diophthalmus* ^

When you find one hibiscus harlequin bug, you normally find a few others! The females of this species lay their eggs in a cluster wrapped around a twig or leaf petiole. Each female then guards these eggs until the metallic blue nymphs hatch out. These nymphs tend to disperse, but rarely go far from each other, staying on the same plant to feed. They feed through their rostrum, which pierces through plant tissue to access fluids inside. They can often be found clustered in the seed pods of bottle trees (*Brachychiton spp.*) or on the undersides of leaves of hibiscus shrubs.

> ***Location:*** *Most common in Queensland, New South Wales, and Victoria with some present in Western Australia and the Northern Territory.*

# STINK BUGS

## FAMILY PENTATOMIDAE

**FACT**
**Stink bugs spray a smelly liquid from holes in the sides of their body.**

Photograph: Dr. Andrew Maynard

### MOTTLED STINK BUG

*Bromocoris souefi* ^

Many bugs are good parents, meaning they take care of their eggs and nymphs. Most insects lay and then leave their eggs, but females of the mottled stink bug will guard over their eggs. This helps prevent the eggs from being eaten or parasitised by predators. Once the eggs hatch into nymphs, this female will stay guarding her babies. The nymphs are vulnerable when they first hatch and cannot eat. Once they moult into their second nymphal instar, they can begin to feed and the mother will finally leave.

> ***Location:*** *Queensland and northern New South Wales.*

### GUM TREE STINK BUGS

*Poecilometis* spp. ^

Gum tree stink bugs can be found across Australia with 38 different species in this genus. Most species are found under the bark of eucalyptus trees where they take shelter. While some species are a brownish-yellow colour and can be difficult to tell apart, others have distinct patterns on their back that look a bit like a face! When disturbed they have a jerky walk and will spray a defensive, stinky liquid. They can also fly away, making a 'buzz' noise when they take off.

> ***Location:*** *Throughout Australia.*

### PREDATORY STINK BUG ^

SUBFAMILY ASOPINAE

While most stink bugs feed on plants, this group are predators and have a thickened rostrum. They feed on soft-bodied prey like caterpillars and beetle larvae. Similar to assassin bugs, this group injects its prey with digestive enzymes before slowly sucking up the liquefied insides. Predatory stink bugs are generalist predators meaning they will feed on whatever insect they can catch. They likely also play an important role in managing herbivorous insect populations.

> ***Location:*** *Throughout Australia.*

# BURROWING BUGS

## FAMILY CYDNIDAE

Burrowing bugs might look a bit like a cockroach or a beetle at a glance, but they're actually true bugs. They usually have smooth, black bodies and digging legs that are well suited to burrowing through soil or sand where they feed on the roots of plants. When it rains, several of these bugs will come to the surface where they will search for a mate.

> ***Location:*** *Throughout Australia.*

**FACT**
**Like stink bugs, they have a defensive spray, but instead of stinking some of them smell like chocolate!**

Photograph: Dr. Andrew Maynard

# SMALL HEADED STINK BUGS

## FAMILY TESSARATOMIDAE

Females can lay up to 42 eggs and will guard over them until they hatch.

### LYCHEE STINK BUG

*Lyramorpha rosea* ^

The flat, shield-shaped nymphs of the lychee stink bug are a strange wonder of the insect world in Australia. They are often brightly coloured with red in the middle and blue border or simply all blue. Adults can also be green or red, two colours that help them blend in with the leaves or trunks of the trees they feed on. Nymphs and adults feed on several native trees including tuckeroo (*Cupaniopsis anacardioides*) and introduced trees like lychees (*Litchi chinensis*). You can see clusters of them on the trunks or branches of trees with large numbers being common when a tree is in poor health.

> ***Location:*** *Coastal regions of southeast Queensland and New South Wales.*

### BRONZE ORANGE BUG

*Musgraveia sulciventris* v

Bronze orange bugs feast on the sap of native citrus trees. These bugs can be seen clustered on a citrus tree, each 'plugged in' to feed with their rostrum. The diet of this species is slightly unfortunate since we grow several citrus trees for us to eat. This includes oranges, mandarins, lemons, and limes. Since this species feeds on the introduced citrus trees as well, it is considered a pest. Aside from the damage that it can cause to the trees, these bugs also have a powerful stink that stings people's eyes and stains skin. Nymphs look like miniature oranges and lemons with their unique, bright colours and round bodies. These colours warn predators of their stink!

**FACT**

**This species can mate for four days! The male and female will stay joined bum-to-bum during this time.**

> ***Location:*** *Southeast Queensland and New South Wales.*

### CARNIVAL BUG

*Peltocopta crassiventris* v

Only the males of the carnival bug live up to their name. They are brightly coloured with yellow, red, and blue spots. Females are pale blue to white with only small streaks of bright colours. Surprisingly, both males and females can be hard to spot! They feed on the undersides of leaves in the rainforest. Females will guard over their eggs covering them with their dome shaped abdomen. Once the eggs hatch, the nymphs will crawl onto the underside of their mother's abdomen where they will stay until they can feed.

> ***Location:*** *Southeast Queensland and northern New South Wales.*

### HAIRY ALECTRYON BUG

*Stilida indecora* v

The hairy alectryon bug is a good mum. Females will guard over the dozens of eggs that they lay. She cannot feed while she guards them and will angle her body over the developing eggs, protecting them from predators and parasitoids. Over time, little eyes appear inside these eggs and soon enough fat, round nymphs hatch out. Like many bugs, the nymphs cannot feed when they first hatch. The female continues to stand guard over these nymphs during this vulnerable time, but there can be so many nymphs that she has to stand on the tips of her tarsi.

> ***Location:*** *Queensland.*

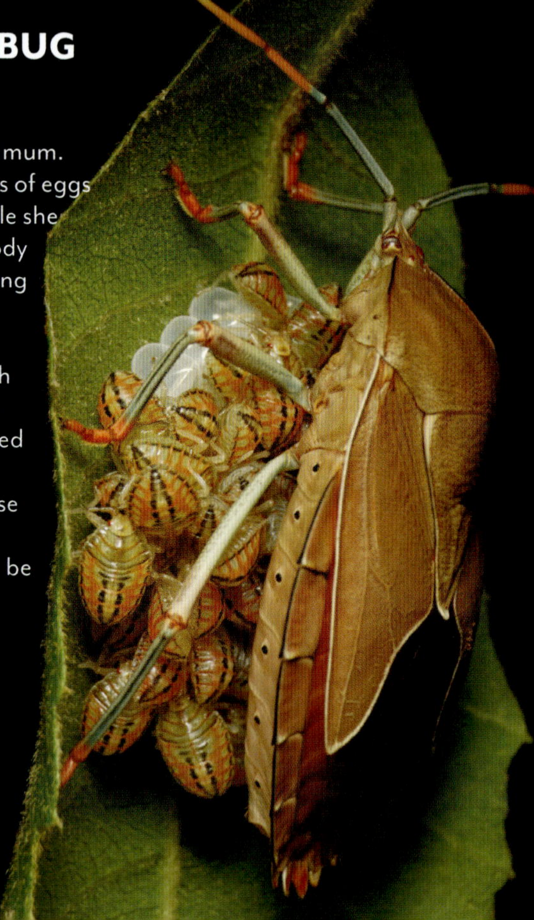

# SPITTLEBUGS

## FAMILY APHROPHORIDAE

Spittle bugs are vulnerable as nymphs. They feed on plant tissue and being out in the open to do this is full of risks. So, this bug uses a special trick: it covers itself in frothy mass that resembles spittle. The spittle comes from excess water that the bug would normally release and a mucilaginous excretion from other parts of its body. Multiple nymphs can be hidden within one spittle covering. Once they moult into adulthood, they leave their spittle days behind them and freely roam around the plant. At this stage they look like a plant thorn or seed and continue to feed on the plant tissue.

> **Location:** *Throughout Australia.*

**FACT**
**Only nymphs cover themselves in spittle, while the adults look like thorns on the plant.**

**Photograph:** Dr. Andrew Maynard.

# TOAD BUGS

## FAMILY GELASTOCORIDAE

### TOAD BUG

*Nerthra alaticollis* ^

If a toad were a bug, it would look like this. These wide, but flat bugs are predators on land and near water. Their bumpy, brown body helps them blend in with the sand that they are normally found amongst. They hop and crawl over the ground in a jerky fashion. While they have lost the ability to fly, these bugs are still successful predators. They have compound eyes and claw-like forelegs for seeing and then catching their prey.

> **Location:** *Southeast Queensland, New South Wales and Victoria.*

# WATER STRIDER

## FAMILY GERRIDAE

### COMMON WATER STRIDER

*Tenagogerris euphrosyne* ⌄

Water striders use the water's surface much like a spider uses its web. These insects can skate across the water thanks to their thin legs, light body, and the surface tension of water. They can also sense the vibrations of struggling insects who have fallen into the water, then quickly skate across the surface to catch this meal. Some water striders also send pulse waves over the water surface to attract mates or to scare off other individuals in their hunting ground. When they mate, water strider females can still hunt, they just carry a male around on their back. This movement can also help them escape predators during such a vulnerable time and allow males to guard their mate from other males. The mating pair pictured here may look like nymphs, but they are adults! Individuals of this species can be winged or wingless as an adult. The wingless forms are thought to be associated with more stable bodies of water, while winged individuals move around to find new water bodies when theirs dry up.

> **Location:** *Throughout Queensland, New South Wales and Victoria.*

CHAPTER 7

# DRAGONFLIES, DAMSELFLIES, AND LACEWINGS

## ORDER ODONATA AND NEUROPTERA

Palemouth dragonflies are agile hunters that can catch their prey mid-flight. You can find them resting near still pools of water.

# INTRODUCTION

Dragonflies and damselflies (Order Odonata) begin their lives as nymphs that hunt in healthy streams and feed on other aquatic insects. Lacewings (Order Neuroptera) are also predators but begin their lives as larvae in the soil or on trees, where they search for prey. In this chapter, we will discover spectacular species from these two different groups and the extraordinary transformations they undertake.

Dragonflies like this common glider begin their lives as predators in the water.

Photograph: Chris Burwell.

Photograph: Chris Burwell.

## GREAT VISION

Dragonflies have some of the best vision among insects. Their large eyes make up most of their head and can judge distances and detect motion up to 1/300th of a second. We look like we're moving in slow-motion to a dragonfly.

## LACEWINGS, ANTLIONS, OWLFLIES, AND MANTIDFLIES

The Order Neuroptera are very diverse both in their appearance and what they eat. Several species in this group are predators, but others can feed on pollen and nectar. Some lacewings are considered important natural predators of pests in our crops, while others may play an important role in their natural ecosystem. Like the dragonflies, both the larvae and adults can be important predators, but this group tends to have special adaptations for camouflage, while dragonflies are agile fliers.

Moth lacewing larvae live in soils and resemble beetle larvae.

## DRAGONFLIES AND DAMSELFLIES

Dragonflies and damselflies are in the same group, Order Odonata and can be told apart by the way that they hold their wings. Dragonflies typically hold their wings out, while damselflies fold their wings behind their body. Dragonflies are also typically larger than damselflies with wider bodies. These insects can lay their eggs in plant tissue, mud, or directly into the water, depending on the species. Damselfly nymphs breathe through gills that can be seen outside their body while dragonfly nymphs have similar gills in their anus or bum. When dragonfly nymphs need to move quickly, they can force water out of their anus to propel forward. They are all predators and have a unique adaptation where their jaws fold out and extend forward to catch prey quickly. Finding dragonfly nymphs can be tricky as they spend this period underwater, but you can always find signs of them. The nymphs will crawl up on nearby plants, rocks, or logs to moult, or shed their exoskeleton and emerge as an adult. You can find these shed skins or moults and inspect them for their unique mouths.

You can find the shed exoskeletons of dragonflies near streams.

# DRAGONFLIES

## ORDER ODONATA, INFRAORDER ANISOPTERA

## CLUB-TAILED DRAGONFLIES

### FAMILY GOMPHIDAE

Photograph: Chris Burwell.

### PALE HUNTER

*Austrogomphus amphiclitus* <

These smaller dragonflies are common along streams and rivers. As adults, they fly rapidly over this area feeding on other insects. During their nymph stage, they live in the water and are voracious predators of other aquatic insects. The females can rapidly lay their eggs in the water by quickly dipping their abdomen in the stream.

> ***Location:*** *Streams and rivers of Queensland and New South Wales.*

## SKIMMERS OR PERCHERS

### FAMILY LIBELLULIDAE

Photograph: Chris Burwell.

### AUSTRALIAN PYGMYFLY

*Nannophya australis* ^

These tiny dragonflies are common in boggy seepages and swamps, where their nymphs feed on other aquatic insects like mosquito larvae. These dragonflies rest in a unique position with their wings down and abdomen raised up. Males of this species have bright red and yellow colours which may help them to attract females.

> ***Location:*** *Queensland, New South Wales, and Victoria.*

### PALEMOUTH

*Brachydiplax denticauda* ^

This species is named after the pale-yellow patch over their mouth. Males are a bright, powder blue when they mature, but females are more dull. They can be found around still waters where they hunt and will lay their eggs. Because of their unique habitat, they can be common around urban areas if there is a large pond.

> ***Location:*** *Western Australia, the Northern Territory, Queensland, and northern New South Wales.*

Photograph: Chris Burwell.

### SCARLET PERCHER

*Diplacodes haematodes* ^

There are several small, red species of dragonflies, but this species is especially vibrant. It can be found along streams, rivers, and still waters. It also prefers to sun itself on rocks and can be seen doing so during the hottest times of the day. The females may look like another species as they are more yellow coloured with darker patches at the tips of their wings.

> ***Location:*** *Throughout Australia, except Tasmania.*

**Photograph:** Chris Burwell.

## GRAPHIC FLUTTERER
*Rhyothemis graphiptera*

The dark patches in the wings of the graphic flutterer may help this dragonfly blend in with its surroundings when it suns itself. They fly in a fluttering pattern, more similar to a butterfly than a dragonfly.

> ***Location:*** *Lakes, ponds, and swamps of Western Australia, the Northern Territory, Queensland, and New South Wales.*

## YELLOW-STRIPED FLUTTERER
*Rhyothemis phyllis*

Like the graphic flutterer, this species also glides as it flies, fluttering like a butterfly. This is likely because of their large wings, each of which are longer than its body. It can rapidly change the direction that it is flying to catch prey, however. This species can be seen commonly around large ponds or swamps.

> ***Location:*** *Western Australia, the Northern Territory, and coastal regions of Queensland, and northern New South Wales.*

# PETALTAIL DRAGONFLIES

## FAMILY PETALURIDAE

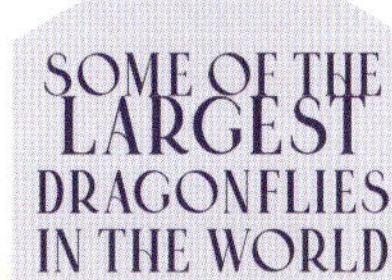


### SOUTH-EASTERN PETALTAIL
*Petalura gigantea* ∨

These dragonflies are named after the petal-like segments on the end of each males' abdomen. They are very large dragonflies and can be found around boggy seepages and swamps. You may hear them flying before you see them as they whirr through the sky. Petaltail nymphs construct tunnels that connect to the stream, filling their burrow with water. They are considered semi-aquatic due to this habit.

> ***Location:*** *New South Wales.*

**Photograph:** Chris Chafer.

**Photograph:** Chris Burwell.

### COASTAL PETALTAIL DRAGONFLY
*Petalura litorea* ∧

This species was only described in 1999 when it was found to be unique from the south-eastern petaltail. It is more slender and usually black. Both species of petaltails live in boggy seepages and swamps where their larvae form burrows or tunnels that fill with water. Both petaltail species are considered endangered in New South Wales due to destruction of their habitat.

> ***Location:*** *Southeast Queensland and northern New South Wales.*

# DAMSELFLIES

ORDER ODONATA, SUBORDER ZYGOPTERA

## AZURE DAMSELFLIES FAMILY LESTOIDEIDAE

Photograph: Chris Burwell.

### TROPICAL ROCKMASTER

*Diphlebia euphoeoides* <

Males of this damselfly are a vibrant blue, while females are more camouflaged greenish brown. This is thought to be a result of females only mating with brightly coloured blue males, driving this characteristic in the population.

> **Location:** *Tropical coast of Queensland.*

### WHITEWATER ROCKMASTER

*Diphlebia lestoides* ⌄

> ***Location:*** *Streams and rivers of coastal New South Wales and Victoria.*

**Both photographs:** Chris Burwell.

## NARROW-WINGED DAMSELFLIES

FAMILY COENAGRIONIDAE

These damselflies can be seen fighting around flowing or still waters like those at a billabong.

### EASTERN BILLABONGFLY

*Austroagrion watsoni* >

Males of these small damselflies are bright blue, while the females are brown to dull yellow in the same regions. This contrast in colour is thought to help females to camouflage as they lay their eggs, while the males need to be more conspicuous. Males need to be showy to attract mates and to fight off other males.

> **Location:** *Still and flowing waters throughout Australia except coastal regions of Western Australia.*

## WIRETAIL DAMSELFLIES

FAMILY ISOSTICTIDAE

### LARGE WIRETAIL

*Labidiosticta vallisi* <

When a male damselfly finds a female to mate with, he will attach to the back of her head using claspers on the end of his abdomen. The two can then fly together, escaping predators and searching for the perfect spot to lay eggs. If the female accepts the male, the pair will also form a 'heart' shape that allows the male to pass over his sperm and fertilise the female's eggs. After mating, females will lay their eggs on branches, logs, or plants near water so that when they hatch, their nymphs can immediately enter the stream.

> **Location:** *Eastern Australia.*

# LACEWINGS, OWFLIES, AND MANTIDFLIES

ORDER NEUROPTERA

## ANTLIONS

FAMILY MYRMELEONTIDAE

Antlion larvae build sand traps to catch ants and other invertebrates that they eat. The antlion larva lays in wait, buried in sand at the base of its funnel-shaped trap. If an ant falls in, the steep sides make it difficult to escape. The antlion larva will catch the ant with its large jaws or mandibles. By building a trap, the antlion has its food come to it.

> **Location:** *Throughout Australia.*

This is the lion beneath the sand – an antlion larva!

## LARGE LACEWINGS

FAMILY NYMPHIDAE

### THE BLUE-EYED LACEWING

*Nymphes myrmeleonides* >

The blue-eyed lacewing is most commonly seen at night, flying like little fairies. The adults are some of the largest lacewings, giving them their other common name: giant orange lacewing. Their body can be 5cm long, while their wings can be over 11cm wide. They fly slowly at night, making them easy to catch. During the day, they will hide on the underside of leaves with their wings neatly folded.

> **Location:** *Coastal areas of Queensland, New South Wales, and Victoria.*

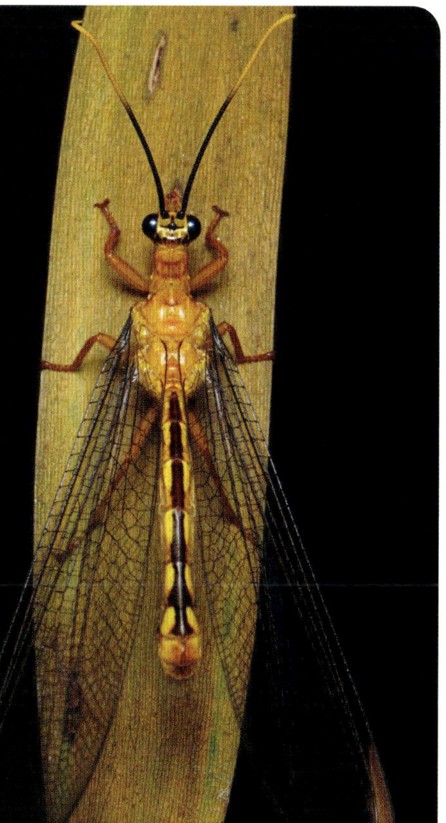

### OSMO LACEWING

*Osmylops* sp. ^

This lacewing nymph is an ambush predator. To be a successful ambush predator, it needs two key traits: to remain hidden from prey and to be able to catch prey quickly. The lacewing's colours match the underside of this leaf, helping it blend in while its open jaws are ready to catch any prey once it comes by. ∨

# MOTH LACEWINGS

## FAMILY ITHONIDAE

### THE MOTH LACEWING

*Ithone fulva* >

Moth lacewings can be found in sandy, coastal habitats. Their nymphs spend their lives in the sand and are thought to be predatory, feeding on the larvae of beetles and other insects which are found in the same habitat. Their nymphs also smell strongly of citronella, making some scientists think that they feed on plants.

> **Location:** *Sandy coastal areas of southeast Queensland.*

## STORY OF THE MOTH LACEWING

The moth lacewing was first thought to live in the water as a nymph. But scientists found adult lacewings on a fence far from any source of water, making them suspect that this lacewing began its life in sand instead. Entomologists, Dr. John Tillyard and Luke Gallard spent many hours digging for these lacewings nymphs in the early 1900s, but all they found were the larvae of scarab beetles. Later on, they were able to collect a few adult moth lacewings which laid eggs. Excited to finally see the nymphs of these lacewings, the entomologists could not believe what they discovered. Strange, soft bodied nymphs that resembled beetle larvae hatched out. The two scientists realised they had seen hundreds of the lacewing larvae, but mistakenly thrown them aside all along!

# GREEN LACEWINGS

## FAMILY CHRYSOPIDAE

Green lacewings hatch from eggs on stalks. These nymphs then begin to hunt. They aren't just the usual hunters though, these lacewings will gather 'trash' from their environment like pieces of leaves, seeds, or even pieces of other insects. They then use this trash pile to cover their body, disguising themselves. Some lacewing larvae are even known to stack the bodies of their prey on their back after feeding on them.

> **Location:** *Throughout Australia.*

# SILKY LACEWINGS

## FAMILY PSYCHOPSIDAE

### BIRD POOP LACEWING

*Psychopsis illidgei* ∨

Little is known about this rare lacewing, but its adults have wings that resemble bird poop. In the day, these lacewings are inactive, hiding their head underneath their wings. While this camouflage can help protect the lacewing from predators, it could also disguise this lacewing from prey. The bird poop pattern on its wings may attract flies and other insects which may be what it likes to eat.

> **Location:** *This species has only been found on rare occasions in southeast Queensland.*

# MANTISFLIES

## FAMILY MANTISPIDAE

### COMMON MANTISFLY

*Ditaxis biseriata* >

These active predators fly to and chase after prey. They have large eyes that help them hunt and unique raptorial forelegs with spikes that help them catch prey. While they look like a mantis, these are lacewings, an entirely different group. This is an example of convergent evolution. Many lacewings are predators like mantids, and raptorial forelegs are very useful to such predators. Each group has uniquely evolved this trait overtime. Most mantisflies are rare, but this species and another (*D. meridiei*) can be found commonly in parks.

**FACT**
**The mantisfly has raptorial forelegs like a mantis, but cannot use these legs to walk!**

> ***Location:*** *Southeast Queensland and northern New South Wales; a similar species can be found in Victoria.*

# OWLFLIES

## FAMILY ASCALAPHIDAE

### YELLOW OWLFLY

*Suhpalacsa flavipes* <

Owlflies have split vision: their compound eyes are each divided in two halves with the top part of the eyes being sensitive to UV light, and the bottom half being able to see both UV and blue-green light. Research suggests that this split vision helps owlflies hunt in low light. The bottom region of the eye is used for broad-focus to first locate their prey, while the top half is used as a fine-focus to pinpoint prey. Owlflies may resemble dragonflies and damselflies (Order Odanata) but are in a separate group called Order Neuroptera. You can tell an owlfly from a dragonfly or damselfly by looking for long, clubbed antennae and their divided eye. If your insect has these, it is most likely an owlfly.

> ***Location:*** *Queensland, New South Wales, and Victoria.*

CHAPTER 8

# GRASSHOPPERS, KATYDIDS AND CRICKETS

## ORDER ORTHOPTERA

Spiny rainforest katydids will come out at after sunset to feed under the safe cover of darkness.

# INTRODUCTION

All grasshoppers, katydids and crickets are part of the Order Orthoptera and can collectively be called Orthopterans. Insects in this group have modified hindlegs for jumping! Their powerful jumps come from a catapult-like structure. They first slowly contract the muscles in their legs and fold their legs in. When they are ready to jump, they quickly release this tension which forces them into the air! Once they have jumped, many grasshoppers and katydids will then fly or glide with their large wings.

**Edible Insects:** Insects pack a lot of protein in a small package and are easy to raise! Crickets can be purchased whole or as powder to add some extra protein to your diet. They often taste quite nutty.

Northern grass pyrgomorph grasshopper (*Atractomorpha similis*)

## FACT

**Many grasshoppers will vomit to defend themselves!**

## NIGHT MUSIC

**Katydids and crickets can call at night by using a stridulatory file on the underside of one of their forewings. They often call to attract mates, leaving males as the main singers.**

## GRASSHOPPERS VS KATYDIDS

Most species of grasshoppers are active during the day and herbivorous, meaning they feed on plants. Katydids and crickets tend to be more active at night and while many species are herbivorous, there are lots of others that are predacious or omnivorous, meaning they can eat anything!

**When an insect moults, it also sheds the lining of its tracheae, which are oxygen-delivering tubes throughout their body.**

32-spotted katydid (*Ephippitytha trigintiduoguttata*)

**Orthopterans need to hear each other when they sing.** They have a specialised organ for hearing called a tympanum, but it is not found on their head. Instead, katydids and crickets have tympanal organs on each of their front legs while grasshoppers have theirs on their abdomen. Can you imagine having your ears on your arms or your belly?

# GRASSHOPPERS

SUBORDER CAELIFERA

## COLOURFUL GRASSHOPPERS

FAMILY PYRGOMORPHIDAE

Photograph: Nick Volpe.

### PAINTED PYRGOMORPH GRASSHOPPER

*Greyacris picta* ^

This beautiful grasshopper is nearly wingless! Adults have lost the ability to fly and are adapted to live in the harsh, arid regions of Australia. It thrives by feeding on the small shrubs that grow here. Its black, red, and white colours also warn predators that it is distasteful. If a predator gets too close, the little hoppers will raise what is left of their short wings to make the message clear before jumping away.

***Locality:** Inland areas of Western Australia and the Northern Territory.*

Photograph: Nick Volpe.

### CHILD OF LIGHTNING

The Jawoyn and Gundjeihmi people of western Arnhem Land call these grasshoppers 'Alyurr' or the children of the lightning man, Namarrgon. In some years, large numbers can be seen at the start of the rainy season.

### ALYURR OR LEICHHARDT'S GRASSHOPPER

*Petasida ephippigera* ^

The other common name for this grasshopper is from the German explorer, Ludwig Leichhardt, who saw great numbers of these grasshoppers when he passed through in 1845. But numbers of these grasshoppers can fluctuate drastically from year to year, with little explanation. Bright red colours usually advertise that an organism is toxic. In the case of this grasshopper, it likely just tastes awful from the *Pityrodia* shrub that it feeds on. Much remains to be known of this grasshopper, including its biology and ecology.

AUSTRALIA

> ***Location:** Arnhem Land, the Northern Territory.*

### NORTHERN GRASS PYRGOMORPH

*Atractomorpha similis* <

This species' peculiar long face make it look more like a blade of grass instead of a grasshopper. It relies on this cryptic appearance to keep it hidden from danger and is not likely to jump away until the last second. If you have the eyes to spot it, you may find this species in your garden. To some, it is considered a pest since it feeds on many garden plants.

> ***Location:** Coastal areas of the Northern Territory, Queensland and New South Wales.*

# SHORT-HORNED GRASSHOPPERS

FAMILY ACRIDIDAE

Photograph: Dave Rentz.

**FACT**

**Locusts are grasshoppers in a different physical phase with longer wings.**

## AUSTRALIAN PLAGUE LOCUST

*Chortoicetes terminifera*

The Australian plague locust can darken fields with their mass migrations. These do not happen every year though and this locust is not always a locust. That is, this species has two growth phases. If grown in an environment with few individuals, it will be in a solitary phase and grow into a grasshopper. However, if there is plenty of food to eat and many nymphs survive, these grasshoppers will grow in a dense population and be in their gregarious phase. These gregarious phase nymphs turn into locusts. Locusts differ from grasshoppers in two main ways. They can have longer wings adapted for flying over long distances and they behave very differently, moving in swarms to find suitable food. That food is often the paddocks of cattle farmers. Their large numbers and food preference have made this native insect species one of the most destructive in Australia!

> ***Location:*** *Naturally occurs in arid regions of Australia, but can migrate during swarming years to every state.*

## CHAMELEON GRASSHOPPER

*Kosciuscola tristis*

On the cold slopes of an alpine habitat, is a turquoise treasure. But it isn't always so blue. When the temperature drops to 10°C, these grasshoppers turn black! This is thought to help them gain extra warmth from the sun early in the morning and in the late afternoon as black absorbs more heat. When the temperatures warm up to 15°C, their turquoise colours begin to shine through! This means that this species changes from black to blue and back again with each warm day. The benefits of this colour change are not known however and only males of this species are capable of it. Perhaps, it is more beneficial to be blue when you can display for a female and black when it gets a bit chilly.

AUSTRALIA

> ***Location:*** *Alpine regions of New South Wales and Victoria.*

CAN CHANGE COLOUR

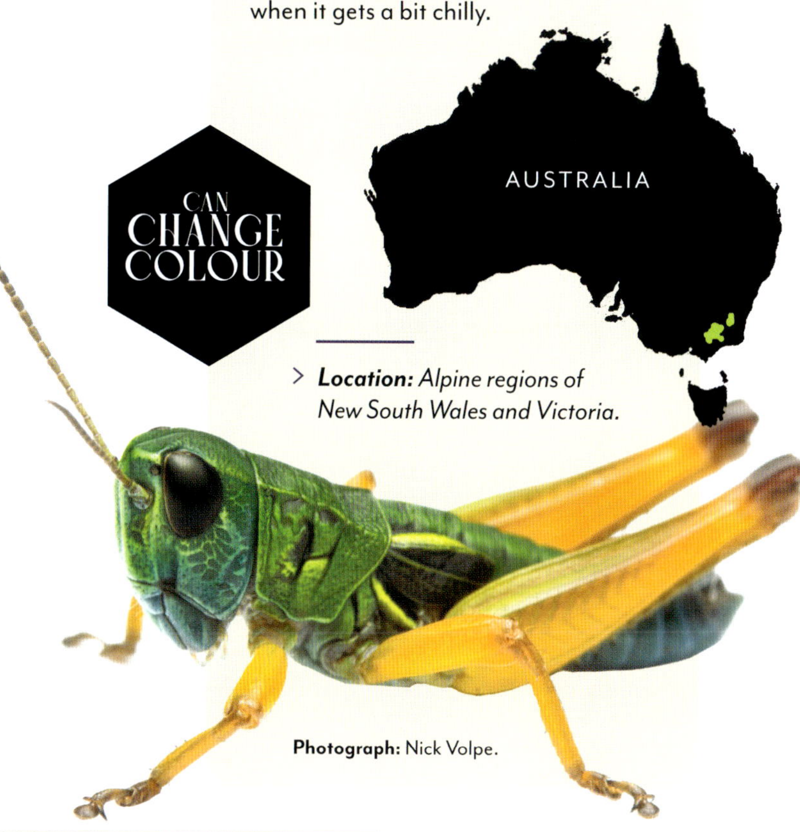
Photograph: Nick Volpe.

## GIANT GRASSHOPPER

*Valanga irregularis* >

This is the largest grasshopper in Australia, with some females reaching 9cm long! They have a variety of colour morphs with the most common pictured here. Each adult has spines on its legs and a powerful jump to help fight off predators. After overwintering as an adult, each female grasshopper will mate and lay about 150 eggs in the soil in early spring. By late spring to mid-summer, young nymphs hatch out and begin eating the leaves of several plants, including many that people grow in home gardens. These grasshopper nymphs are green with a black stripe and many spots, helping them blend in with their food. Once they have grown large enough, these grasshoppers will disperse and are often only found alone. On sunny winter afternoons, the large adults can be spotted sunning themselves on leaves. They are widely dispersed across Australia, and their generalist diet has led to their success in each habitat, including our own backyards.

> **Location:** *Coastal areas of Western Australia, the Northern Territory, Queensland and New South Wales.*

## SPOTTED SPUR-THROATED LOCUST

*Austracris basalis* ^

Australia is full of dry habitats where grasshoppers have thrived. This species subsists on the little vegetation that is available. But in years with heavy rainfall and a lot of plant growth, this species and others can grow to large numbers. This is when they enter their gregarious phase and become locusts. They look and behave differently, swarming and feasting on their favourite plants. This native grasshopper closely resembles another Australian species called the spur-throated locust (*Austracris guttulosa*) which is considered a major pest when its populations swarm as they can feed on important pasture for cattle.

> **Location:** *The Northern Territory and northern Queensland.*

# PYGMY GRASSHOPPERS

FAMILY TETRIGIDAE

## STREAM JUMPER GRASSHOPPER

*Tetrix* sp. v

Get your magnifying glass out for these little jumpers! These tiny grasshoppers live in the leaf litter near streams where they are nearly invisible. If you accidentally step close to them, you may see one jump up like popcorn. Keep your eye trained on them because it can be very difficult to find them again.

> **Location:** *Southeast Queensland, New South Wales, Victoria, Tasmania and South Australia.*

**FACT**

**Grasshoppers in this group are usually less than 2cm long!**

## FAMILY TETTIGONIIDAE

**Photograph:** Nick Volpe.

# CONE-HEADED KATYDIDS

## SUBFAMILY CONOCEPHALINAE

### BLACK-FOOTED KATYDID

*Metholce nigritarsis* ^

A fast-paced noise may be heard from the tops of trees during the day or on warm nights. Climb up the tree and you may find a true treasure of Australia: the black-footed katydid. While they come in different colours, some adults resemble a leaf-footed bug nymph (Family Coreidae). If its bright colours do not deter a predator, the katydid also has a startle display where it lifts its pink hindwings. They lead an entirely colourful life, starting out as blood-red nymphs that look toxic to predators. If you live within the range of this lovely insect, keep your eyes and ears on the lookout for it.

> **Location:** *Southeast Queensland into New South Wales, Victoria, South Australia and some sightings in Western Australia.*

### DESTRUCTIVE KATYDID

*Austrosalomona destructor* <

Have you noticed someone taking a bite out of your favourite orchid? If you live in northern Queensland, the culprit may be a hungry, destructive katydid. While it feeds on a wide variety of plants, this katydid is most known for the damage it can cause to prized plants like orchids. They are only active at night, when they come out to feedon seeds, fruits, and flowers or to serenade the females. If the opportunity arises, this species can also prey on other insects. Lime green or gold, this species can come in many colours.

> **Location:** *Tropical North Queensland.*

### SPINE-HEADED KATYDID

*Nicsara spuria* ^

A rhythmic call can be heard in the eucalypt woodland at night and if you follow it, you may find a katydid like this one. These katydids are nocturnal and often call in groups to amplify their sound. They also are not picky eaters. They are omnivorous, feeding on flowers, fruits, and anything they find that suits. Once the sun rises, their music festival is over, and these katydids will hide in the branches or under bark with their legs outstretched.

> **Location:** *Found in northern parts of Western Australia, the Northern Territory and throughout Queensland and New South Wales.*

Its unique patterns and spikes make this katydid one of the best camouflaged insects.

# FALSE LEAF KATYDIDS

## SUBFAMILY PSEUDOPHYLLINAE

**FACT**
Katydid calls are specific to each species. Scientists can use these calls to monitor and identify katydids.

### SPINY RAINFOREST KATYDIDS

*Phricta* spp. <

Life is hard when you're a tasty katydid. Several birds hunt the spiny rainforest katydid which hides during the day on the bark of trees. It almost perfectly blends in with mossy tree bark and will lay flat and motionless on the tree. When clever birds see past this pose, the katydid has another trick in store. It will drop, then raise its front legs and wings. Spots on its legs resemble eyes, making the katydid look like a larger, more intimidating animal rather than a meal.

> ***Location:*** *Coastal regions of Queensland and northern New South Wales.*

# LONG LEGGED KATYDIDS

## SUBFAMILY MECOPODINAE

### QUEENSLAND PALM KATYDID

*Segestidea queenslandica* >

Amongst the native palms of Tropical North Queensland is one of the largest species of katydids found in Australia. It rests during the day, camouflaged like a dead leaf among the palm fronds. Males of this species are very rare, but this is no issue for females. If they cannot find a mate, females can reproduce through parthenogenesis where their unfertilised eggs simply hatch into clones of the mother. This means all her nymphs will be female! Even though it is so large, this species does not have a painful bite. This is because its mouth is modified to eat the narrow palm leaves and cannot open wide enough to bite us.

> ***Location:*** *Tropical North Queensland.*

# LEAF KATYDIDS

## SUBFAMILY PHANEROPTERINAE

### 32-SPOTTED KATYDID

*Ephippitytha trigintiduoguttata* >

The 32-spotted katydid is common in urban areas of eastern Australia, but often calls from high in the treetops. It sounds like someone saying, 'psssst!' These sounds are from males rubbing the bases of their wings together to attract females. Once mated, the female glues strange, flattened eggs to twigs and these later hatch into small, black ant-like nymphs. They turn green as they grow, and adults can have 32 spots – give or take a few!

> ***Location:*** *Throughout Queensland, New South Wales, Victoria and South Australia.*

## AUSTRALIAN LEAF KATYDIDS

*Ozphyllum* spp. >

These katydids spend their days pretending to be leaves. They will rest in a cryptic posture, where their head is hidden with their leaf-like wings up. At night, these katydids forage in the rainforest where they are known to feed on plants, but they can also make their way into your garden and feed on ivy! They do not begin life as miniature leaves though, instead their nymphs are very colourful with reds, blues, whites, and blacks. Nymphs may be very active as they search for the right place to feed.

> ***Location:*** *Coastal regions of Queensland.*

**Search for legs attached to a leaf and you may spot this katydid.**

**Growth of mountain katydid nymphs.**

**Photograph:** Nick Volpe.

## PINK-STRIPE GARDEN KATYDID

*Caedicia* sp. v

This beautiful group of katydids are common and species can be found in nearly every terrestrial habitat from rainforests to deserts! Their nymphs look very different from the adults, changing colour as they grow older. Some nymphs blend in well with the flowers that they feed on, while others can look like leaves. Australia is home to over 30 species of *Caedicia*, with at least 30 more left to be described to science! A future taxonomist will resolve this group, and describe new species so we can begin to appreciate this diverse group.

> ***Location:*** *Throughout Australia.*

### FACT

**Katydids can be predators, herbivores, and even pollinators!**

**Several species of katydids have yet to be named and described.**

## MOUNTAIN KATYDID

*Acripeza reticulata* ^

Mountain katydids can be difficult to see at first. The round females and long-winged males hide next to the bark of dark trees or dead leaves, where they perfectly blend in. While males can fly, females cannot. Frankly, they can hardly jump and have a clumsy walk. But these katydids do have one trick up their sleeves if their camouflage fails them: a flash of their blue and red bum! Both males and females have this display, but it is especially vibrant on the girls. These katydids also exude droplets of a nasty liquid from their abdomen. Together, this says to predators: you do not want to eat me. Their nymphs are black and resemble ants when they are young. While these nymphs do not have a brightly coloured bum, they can inflate their neck which has an orange band. These colours are also meant to warn predators that the katydid is toxic or at least foul tasting.

> ***Location:*** *Patchy distribution through Queensland, New South Wales, Victoria and Tasmania.*

# POLLEN KATYDIDS

## SUBFAMILY ZAPROCHILINAE

### AUSTRALIAN TWIG KATYDID

*Zaprochilus australis* ^

Twig katydids strongly resemble stick insects and benefit from this camouflage. They hold their stick-like wings at a 45-degree angle, making them look like the corner of a twig. They are active at night, delicately feeding on the nectar and pollen of flowers. Their narrow face is well-made for this, allowing them to reach inside the flowers to sip at the nectar.

> **Location:** *Southeast Queensland, New South Wales, Victoria, Tasmania, South Australia and Western Australia.*

### BALSAM BEAST

*Anthophiloptera dryas* >

This banana-coloured katydid began its life as a green nymph. Nymphs mimic leaves and hide until they get a chance to feast on pollen and honey from flowers. As they feed, the small hairs on their body, called setae, collect pollen. They then transport this pollen to other flowers, pollinating them.

> **Location:** *East coast of Australia.*

Photograph: Dr. Andrew Maynard.

# KING CRICKETS

## FAMILY ANOSTOSTOMATIDAE

### GIANT KING CRICKET

*Anostostoma australasiae* ^

These enormous crickets crawl out from their underground burrows on wet nights. They forage in the surrounding rainforest for their favourite foods: rotten fruit and live insects! Males of this species have extraordinarily long jaws that are not seen in other king crickets in Australia. No one knows what they do with these large jaws, as the species here is poorly studied. However, the giant king cricket is closely related to the wētās of New Zealand. A similar species there, called the Mercury Islands tusked wētās (*Motuweta isolata*) also has males with large jaws. These males fight with each other using these jaws when they emerge from their burrows. They fight to defend their burrow or access a female.

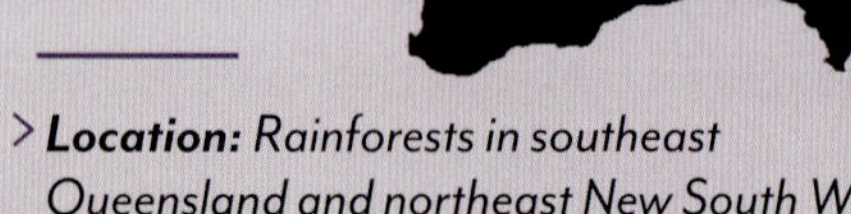


> **Location:** *Rainforests in southeast Queensland and northeast New South Wales.*

# CAMEL CRICKETS OR CAVE WETAS

## FAMILY RHAPHIDOPHORIDAE

This family of unique crickets all have long legs and antennae and a small, hunched body. Their hunched form resembles the humps on a camel's back. All camel crickets are nocturnal, meaning they come out at night. Many species live in caves and are commonly known as cave wētās although they are not in the same group as the true New Zealand wētās (Family Anostostomatidae). Others live in forests, where they often hide in animal burrows, or under stones and logs. Some can even be found in your basement!

> **Location:** *Throughout Australia.*

# CRICKETS

## FAMILY GRYLLIDAE

### WINTRENA METEOR CRICKET

*Myara wintrena* ^

These crickets are named after their ability to shoot off like a meteor and escape. Males of this species begin singing in the late afternoon and continue into the night. They often sing from clumps of leaves at first but will move to a more exposed perch as night falls.

> **Location:** *Queensland.*

### COMMON TREE CRICKET

*Oecanthus angustus* >

The common tree cricket does not live in trees at all! Instead, it lives in grasses where the males make a nice trilling call at night. Males will sing together in groups for several minutes, then move to a new patch of grass and sing again. Females can be found wherever the males are singing and are likely drawn in by the lovely chorus. These crickets are delicate, straw-coloured creatures that are light enough to walk on the blades of grass. They are often found alongside the road at night when their singing begins.

> ***Location:** Found in all states except Tasmania.*

# RASPY CRICKETS

## FAMILY GRYLLACRIDIDAE

PRODUCE THEIR OWN SILK

If you find a raspy cricket, watch out! These little insects have a painful bite. Most species are omnivorous, meaning they can feed on anything, but several species are also carnivorous. These predator species have large, sharp mandibles for catching and then chewing up their prey. During the day, they often hide in curled leaves or under bark and come out at night to hunt.

> **Location:** *Throughout Australia.*

# COOLOOLA MONSTERS

## FAMILY COOLOOLIDAE

### COOLOOLA MONSTER

*Cooloola* sp. v

Not a cricket or a grasshopper, but a monster! This group of insects was only discovered in the 1980s. They are built for living underground, with a hunched body and shovel-like legs for digging through the sand. While they look awkward, these guys are quick and voracious predators. They are known to gobble up beetle grubs and other invertebrates that hide in the sand. Female Cooloola monsters are even thought to spend their entire lives below ground!

**FACT**

**Cooloola monsters are extremely rare and only found in Queensland!**

> **Location:** *Sandy habitats of southeast Queensland.*

CHAPTER 9

# MANTISES AND COCKROACHES

## ORDER MANTODEA AND BLATTODEA

The giant forest cockroach looks like a walking leaf. It comes out at night to feed on fungus and bird droppings on leaves like a janitor of the forest.

# INTRODUCTION

While they all may look very different, mantises (Order Mantodea) are most closely related to cockroaches and termites (Order Blattodea). Both mantises and cockroaches lay their eggs in an ootheca or egg case. Mantises are predators with specially adapted raptorial forelegs. These spikey front legs resemble jaws and can crush the mantises' prey as it eats it. Cockroaches and termites recycle nutrients like those found in dead wood or leaves. Their bodies are often softer and they have specialised gut microbiome to help them digest different materials. In this chapter, you'll meet the heaviest, prettiest, and most important species of mantises and cockroaches.

Rainbow mantises hunt among gum leaves.

## FACT

Mantises are often called, 'praying mantises' after the way that they keep their raptorial forelegs folded. Instead of praying, they are often just hiding!

## OOTHECA <

For cockroaches, their ootheca comes in a hard case that resembles a clutch purse. Some species can even carry this large, leathery egg case around! They awkwardly clench the ootheca inside their bum until they find a suitable place to put it. Many cockroaches then glue this ootheca to a tree before hiding it under pieces of bark while others simply bury it in the ground.

Female boxer bark mantis

Mantises can have special markings on their raptorial forelegs. These are often used for startle displays.

**Mantis oothecas** start as a frothy secretion before they dry and harden. Some resemble a sponge and can have over 100 nymphs hatch out! Newly hatched nymphs cannot feed, so they moult immediately. If they do not disperse quickly, they might eat each other! >

# MANTISES

ORDER MANTODEA

## BARK MANTISES

FAMILY AMORPHOSCELIDAE

### BOXER BARK MANTIS

*Paraoxypilus verreauxii* >

You may not see this mantis until it is right in front of you! That is because they blend in perfectly with the bark of trees where they hunt for their prey. This species moves quickly over the bark and flexes its raptorial forelegs, much like a boxer would bounce his fists. When they feel threatened, they will hold out their forelegs to make themselves seem larger and display an otherwise hidden red, white, and black pattern.

> **Location:** *Northern Queensland.*

### SOUTHERN BOXER BARK MANTIS

*Paraoxypilus tasmaniensis* ^

Male boxer mantises have long wings and can fly, while females have no wings and a round body. These differences help the males fly to females, while females with a larger body can lay more eggs and hide along the bark. Even the eyes of these mantises look like bark.

> **Location:** *Coastal regions of southeast Queensland, New South Wales, Victoria, Tasmania, South Australia and Western Australia.*

## GARDEN MANTISES

FAMILY MANTIDAE

### AUSTRALIAN GARDEN MANTIS

*Orthodera ministralis* >

These small green mantises often rest with their raptorial forelegs folded in. They blend in well with a variety of plants, where they hunt for prey. Inside their folded legs is a secret: a blue spot that they can display when they feel threatened. This species is common in a variety of habitats, particularly open forests and can be found in several gardens.

> **Location:** *Coastal regions throughout Australia.*

**FACT**

**The eggs of these mantises can be parasitised by wasps! To get the eggs as soon as they are laid, wasps will rest on the female mantis until she lays her eggs.**

## AUSTRALIAN STICK MANTIS

*Archimantis* spp. <

IT EATS CICADAS!

This group has some of the longest mantises in Australia. They can be spotted hunting prey on trees or even under lights that attract other insects. They often hang on the ends of branches where they blend in and can easily catch unsuspecting prey. They catch large insects like cicadas with their strong raptorial forelegs. These legs then hold their prey as they 'dig in'. Females are much larger than males and have shorter wings that only cover half of their abdomen, while males have full-length wings and can fly. There are several species in Australia, including the Northern Stick Mantis (*Archimantis armata*) pictured here. All species resemble large sticks and can be tricky to spot!

^ ***Location:*** *All states except Tasmania.*

## FALSE GARDEN MANTIS

*Pseudomantis albofimbriata* >

**MUNCHING MANTISES!**

**Females of the false garden mantis will sometimes eat their mates!**

As you have learned so far, mantis females tend to have shorter wings and larger bodies while males are smaller with longer wings. Researchers have found that those differences are beneficial in this species. Heavier females can lay more eggs, while males need to be light with long wings to find females. However, it is dangerous to be a male false garden mantis: the females sometimes eat the males! This is more likely to happen when a female is hungry. Male mantises find females by 'smelling' them out, but they cannot smell if a female is hungry or not. When they finally find a female, they can tell if she might be hungry. If she is, they risk being eaten to mate with her. Some males take this risk and may get eaten before they even get a chance to mate!

> ***Location:*** *Coastal regions of Queensland, New South Wales, Victoria, Tasmania and South Australia.*

Sitting and waiting for her meal. Will it be prey or a male trying to mate?

### GIANT RAINFOREST MANTIS

*Hierodula majuscula* ∨

Females of this rainforest giant can be over seven centimetres long! They hunt in their rainforest homes for other invertebrates, but some large females can also hunt geckos and frogs! Adults are mostly green, with red and black patterns inside their raptorial forelegs. When under threat, they fold these legs near their face to make themselves appear like the open mouth of a large animal!

> **Location:** *Northern Queensland.*

**Photograph by:** Alamy.

### RAINBOW MANTIS

*Sphodropoda quinquedens*

While they are not rainbow coloured, this species does come in a variety of colours including green, red, and brown. They have toothed raptorial forelegs like most mantises, alongside a second set of deadly internal spines on their forelegs. These spines help them crush their prey while also protecting the mantis from prey that may bite back. When threatened, this species is more likely to flatten itself against whatever it is on. In a way, it pretends it does not exist, hoping the threat will go away too.

> **Location:** *Northern coastal areas of Queensland and the Northern Territory.*

# NANO MANTISES

## FAMILY NANOMANTIDAE

### LICHEN MANTIS

*Calofulcinia oxynota* ∨

There is danger among the lichen! This mantis blends in perfectly with the lichen on trees, helping it sneak up on prey. Despite its tiny size, this female is fully grown! Males are not much bigger, but they do have full wings that allow them to fly. Being small is best for this species as they can easily hide in their micro-habitat on the tree.

> **Location:** *Northern Queensland.*

**Photograph:** Dr. Andrew Maynard.

This species guards over its eggs until they hatch!

### NET-WINGED MANTIS

*Neomantis australis* <

This species uses a different strategy for blending in. Instead of looking like a stick or moss, it resembles a leaf! The wide, flat wings of females help them blend in with the underside of leaves where they lay their small ootheca. The female will then guard over these eggs instead of leaving them as most mantises do. This can help protect them from parasites and predators. When the young nymphs hatch out, their mother is also there to help them!

> **Location:** *Northern coastal areas of Queensland.*

# COCKROACHES

## ORDER BLATTODEA

Of all insects, cockroaches may have the worst reputation. Their name is usually met with disgust based on the species we are most familiar with: the pests that live in our houses. But Australia is home to a remarkable diversity of cockroaches that are critical to recycling nutrients in the environment and some that are quite beautiful. Some of the most beautiful cockroaches can be found in Western Australia where the arid conditions have been met with uniquely adapted and colourful species. Roaches can also eat leaf litter, pollen, and even decaying wood! Cockroaches occupy all terrestrial habitats, with several unique species living in caves and feeding on bat guano or poop!

This cockroach can hiss when disturbed! The sound is made by the body compressing and forcing air out of its rear end.

**FACT**

Giant burrowing cockroaches are great parents. The female gives birth to 15-30 live young and cares for them for a year!

# GIANT COCKROACHES

## FAMILY BLABERIDAE

### GIANT BURROWING COCKROACH

*Macropanesthia rhinoceros* >

As their name suggests, the giant burrowing cockroach spends its life underground in deep spiral burrows and is a true giant. It is the heaviest cockroach in the world with the record female weighing over 30g! This size is impressive considering its limited diet of dead, dry leaves, which it drags into its burrow at night. This diet helps them live in the unique habitat of open forests in inland regions of northern Queensland. Sadly, their underground life makes them difficult to find, but they tend to come to the surface after summer rains.

> **Location:** *Coastal and inland regions of northern Queensland.*

### NOOSA BURROWING COCKROACH

*Geoscapheus crenulatus* ^

Thousands of years ago, ancestors of these cockroaches spread to New Guinea and Australia. They are thought to have fed on decaying wood, but over these few thousand years, Australia became more and more arid. This environmental change is thought to have driven this species to live in underground burrows. Today, this is where we find them, or at least dig them out from! This species, like others in its genus feed on leaf litter. At night, these cockroaches will crawl to the surface and then drag dried leaves back into their sandy burrow. It then munches away at these leaves, safely below ground.

> **Location:** *Noosa and K'gari, Queensland.*

## NOOSA BURROWING COCKROACH BUDDY

Unknown species ^

This species can only be found in one place: the burrow of the Noosa burrowing cockroach. These smaller cockroaches are poorly studied, with these photographed individuals being impossible to identify currently. They are thought to feed on the poop of the larger burrowing cockroach. They may also gain protection in the large burrows that their 'buddy' digs out for them. Several of these cockroaches can be found in one burrow.

> **Location:** *Burrows of Geoscapheus crenulatus in Queensland.*

**FACT**
**Cockroaches are important nutrient recyclers, breaking down wood, leaf litter, and even poo!**

## LEAF LITTER SAND COCKROACH

*Calolampra* sp. v

This species is a relative of the Noosa burrowing cockroach buddy. Instead of living underground, this species takes shelter under bark or logs during the day and comes out at night to forage. It eats dead, dry leaves on the forest floor and can help recycle these nutrients which would otherwise take a long time to break down. The mottled patterns on this cockroach help camouflage it amongst the leaf litter. These cockroaches need this camouflage to protect them from the many frogs that eat them!

> **Location:** *Throughout Australia.*

## GIANT FOREST COCKROACH

*Rhabdoblatta* sp. v

This is one of the largest cockroaches that you will find in Australia, but you must go out at night to see it. During the day, this cockroach is virtually invisible amongst the leaves. Its large wings and flat body make it look like a large, dead leaf. At night, it is more active, foraging for fungus, bird droppings, and other materials on leaves.

> **Location:** *Coastal regions of Queensland, New South Wales and Victoria.*

## SURINAM COCKROACH

*Pycnoscelus surinamensis* v

This species is likely originally from South America but has established on the east coast of Australia where it lives in compost bins. Males of this species are very rarely found, making many entomologists think that it is a parthenogenetic species or one that reproduces from only females. The female of this species carries around her ootheca. When it hatches, the nymphs eat the egg case and then crawl out of their mother, making it look like she has given live birth. The nymphs then feed on fluids called exudates from their mother.

> **Location:** *Coastal regions of Queensland and New South Wales.*

## TRILOBITE COCKROACHES

*Laxta* spp. >

Females of this group resemble the extinct marine arthropods, trilobites, while males have wings. These cockroaches are extremely flat and will hide under eucalyptus bark during the day. If you peel away this bark, you may uncover a group of them. They often return to the same site after foraging at night.

> **Location:** *Coastal regions of Queensland and New South Wales.*

# COMMON COCKROACHES

## FAMILY BLATTIDAE

### TRAVELLING METHANA COCKROACH

*Methana marginalis* <

These common, but lovely roaches are most frequently found near heavily forested areas and are only active at night. During the day, they tend to hide in any nearby crevices, including some of our sheds and boxes. This sneaky behaviour is why this species is thought to have been accidentally introduced to Norfolk Island where it is now a minor pest in gardens. Each female can lay 16 ootheca, each of which may hatch into several young cockroaches.

> **Location:** *Coastal regions of Queensland and Norfolk Island.*

**Photograph:** Dave Rentz.

### MITCHELL'S DIURNAL COCKROACH

*Polyzosteria mitchelli* ^

Is this most beautiful cockroach on the planet? This species can be found in many arid regions of Australia, but it can have slightly different colours depending on where it is found. These bright colours warn predators of the toxic fluid that they can squirt out if disturbed. Females can carry their ootheca until they find the right place to dig a hole and then bury the ootheca. This likely protects the egg case from the extreme temperatures found in their environment. True to their name, they are most active at dawn and dusk when they can be seen crawling on the ground.

> **Location:** *Arid regions of Western Australia, South Australia and New South Wales.*

### SLOANE'S NORTHERN WINGLESS COCKROACH

*Cosmozosteria sloanei* >

These cockroaches are common in coastal tropical regions of Australia. They are diurnal, or active at dawn and dusk when they come out to feed on leaf litter and bird droppings. They often rest on low foliage or can be found under logs as well. This species buries its ootheca in sand and sometimes within bark, which likely helps protect it from parasitoid wasps and extreme heat.

> **Location:** *Eastern regions of Queensland.*

# SMALL COCKROACHES

## FAMILY ECTOBIIDAE

### PANDANUS COCKROACH

*Megamareta phaneropyga* >

These golden little cockroaches hide during the day in the spiky leaf bases of Pandanus plants where they are protected from predators and the harsh sun. At night, they crawl out, but instead of eating the leaves, they feed on anything that has fallen on the leaves. In a way, they are the janitor of the Pandanus and surrounding plants, cleaning the leaves of any debris that this species finds tasty. This species also has uniquely clear wings and their young often stay in the same plant as the parents – if there is room!

> **Location:** *Throughout Queensland.*

**Photograph:** Dave Rentz.

# TERMITES

## INFRAORDER ISOPTERA

Although they are commonly called white ants, termites are unrelated to ants and have an incomplete life cycle, growing from nymphs into adults. In fact, termites are most closely related to cockroaches. Termites are small, pale, soft-bodied insects with a variety of body forms, called castes. These castes include small, soft-bodied workers, large, pointy-headed soldiers, and an enormous queen. Once a year, they can also produce a special caste of reproductive termites that have wings and can fly. You can see large numbers of these on warm, humid nights.

### FACT

Termites will vibrate to talk to each other! They can also use these vibrations to find the best wood to eat.

**Photograph:** Stephen Zozaya.

MOST TERMITES ARE BLIND

The soft-bodied worker maintains the nest, while a large-headed soldier defends it.

The author, Jessa, sitting in an old termite mound.

Ecologically, termites are critical to supporting other organisms. They are an important food resource for many animals including echidnas and the endangered numbat. They also help recycle nutrients in their environment, mainly from breaking down dead timber. In some cases, they can be pests – like when they try to recycle our homes!

### TERMITE TRAITS

Termites have two traits that have been key to their success. First, they can digest wood. Wood is made of cellulose, which is very difficult to digest and gain nutrients from. Termites have solved this issue with the thousands of microbes in their gut that break down this cellulose and produce nutrients in the process. Termites gain these microbes when they are young nymphs, and an adult termite feeds them a bit of microbe-filled vomit!

Second, termites live in large social colonies. Their nests are often found underground with some building large earthen mounds that are home to thousands of individuals. Nests like these mounds help protect the delicate termites from predators and drying out. Their unique nests have allowed them to survive in several habitats, from moist rainforests to the dry deserts.

# TRUE TERMITES

## FAMILY TERMITIDAE

### CATHEDRAL TERMITES

*Nasutitermes triodiae* >

Cathedral termites are named after their impressive, bulky mounds. They build this tough mound out of a mix of their saliva, poop, mud, and plant material, which holds strong through cyclones. The mound also protects the termites from the extreme heat! It has its own form of air-conditioning where hollow columns allow air from the cooler soil below ground to circulate with the warm air from the colony. This species is common in arid habitats and feeds on grasses like kangaroo grass (*Themeda triandra*). Soldiers defend the nest with their fontanellar gun which shoots out a glue-like material over several centimetres. This glue is thought to entangle or irritate any potential invaders.

Soldiers of this species have an elongated, tubular snout called a nasus, which has a special weapon called a fontanellar gun!

> ***Location:*** *Arid regions of Western Australia, the Northern Territory and Queensland.*

**Photograph:** Nick Volpe.

**FACT**

**Cathedral termite mounds can be over 8m tall!**

**Photograph:** Nick Volpe.

### MAGNETIC TERMITES

*Amitermes meridionalis* <

These termite mounds resemble tombstones. The wide faces of these mounds face east and west, while the narrow ends point north and south. But who gave these termites a compass? These termites have magnetoreception or the ability to sense Earth's magnetic fields. This allows them to construct their unique, thin mounds. But why build a nest like this? The orientation and structure of these mounds helps the termites keep a stable temperature inside the nest. Unlike the cathedral termites, this species lives on floodplains and cannot build underground chambers to cool their nest. Instead, their mound acts as their temperature control. The mound absorbs heat from the sun when it rises in the east and sets in the west. At mid-day, the colony stays cool by not absorbing the heat from the sun which shines straight down.

> ***Location:*** *The Northern Territory.*

CHAPTER 10

# STICK AND LEAF INSECTS

## ORDER PHASMATODEA

Male dancing leaf insects have long, hairy antennae to help them smell out their female counterparts.

## INTRODUCTION

Stick and leaf insects are often overlooked. Their cryptic appearance helps keep them safe from predators, with species blending in perfectly with leaves, twigs, or even branches. Certain species of phasmids are also the longest insects in the world. Few species have wings capable of flight, while others are completely wingless. Their unique form is also seen in their seed-like eggs. Nymphs that hatch out can resemble ants or small versions of the adult. Here, you'll meet the longest, smelliest, and strangest phasmids of Australia

Dancing leaf insects eat and look like leaves with their flat, green body.

### LIMB LOSS?

Stick insects easily drop their legs when under threat. This can help them escape a predator when caught. If they are still young when they lose a limb, they can regrow it too. This regrowth happens between each moult, so if a young nymph has several moults before it will become an adult, then it can regrow a lost limb in that time. The regrown limb is typically smaller than those retained. Adults that lose legs, however, cannot regrow them as they unfortunately have no moults left.

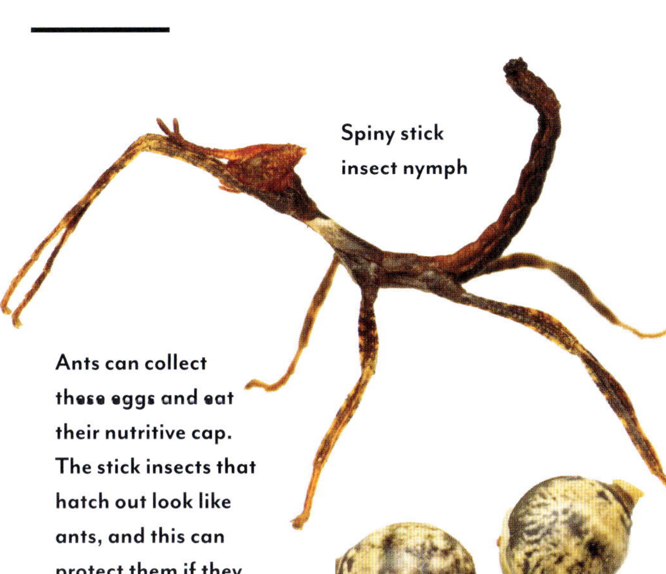

Spiny stick insect nymph

Ants can collect these eggs and eat their nutritive cap. The stick insects that hatch out look like ants, and this can protect them if they hatch in an ant nest! >

### COLOUR COUNTS >

Stick insects rely on their camouflage to avoid being eaten by predators. The same species can be found in a variety of colours, like the spiny stick insect (*Extatosoma tiaratum*) which is normally tan or brown. It can also be red, green, or even black and white! These different colours help them blend in with leaves, seed pods, and even lichen.

< Children's stick insect (*Tropidoderus childrenii*)

Some spiny stick insects can blend in with lichen!

### MALES ARE NOT NECESSARY IN THE PHASMID WORLD

Most female phasmids can lay unfertilised eggs that will still hatch! This is a type of reproduction called parthenogenesis, where females reproduce by themselves. When this happens, only female phasmids are produced. If a female cannot find a mate, she can still reproduce. The males are not as fortunate.

# SPINDLY STICK INSECTS

## FAMILY DIAPHEROMERIDAE

### TINY STICK INSECTS

*Pachymorpha* spp. >

Species within this genus are some of the smallest stick insects in Australia. They can be found in rainforests, often on the ground or low shrubs. Both males and females are wingless, with stout bodies, short antennae and very thin legs. They are active at night and have been seen gluing their eggs to twigs and small leaves. This may help the eggs avoid getting too wet and growing mould, but this has not been studied. When they first hatch, the nymphs are green, but will steadily turn tan to dark brown as they grow older. Only three species of *Pachymorpha* have been described, but several others remain unnamed. This is due to the need for taxonomists in Australia to help describe and study our native species.

> ***Location:*** *East coast of Australia and Victoria.*

**Phasmids have finger-like projections around their mouth for holding leaves.**

**See how this species transforms as it grows.**

### CYCLONE LARRY STICK INSECT

*Sipyloidea larryi* ∨

These stick insects thrive in rainforests where they come out at night to feed. Adults of this slender species can fly well and do so to escape predators. It is named after a cyclone that damaged some of its rainforest habitat in 2006.

> ***Location:*** *Tropical North Queensland.*

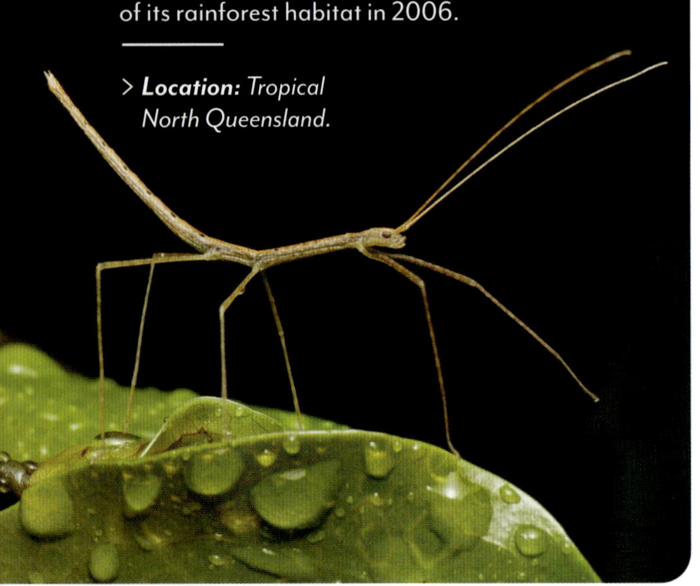

**Both photographs:** Dave Rentz.

### NORTHERN DESERT STICK INSECT

*Sipyloidea nelida* ∧

This desert stick insect has a unique adaptation to survive in its arid environment. Females lay their eggs in the bark of trees including, mulga (*Acacia aneura*) and desert cassia (*Cassia nemophila*). Their eggs are coated with a two-layered membrane that bursts to form a ring of hairs that look like the head of a dandelion. These hairs help the egg absorb any nearby moisture and prevent them from drying out in the desert.

> ***Location:*** *Arid regions of the Northern Territory, South Australia, and Western Australia.*

# STICK INSECTS
FAMILY PHASMATIDAE

> **FACT**
> This species is endangered, but it was once thought to be extinct!

# TREE LOBSTERS
SUBFAMILY EURYCANTHINAE

Male

Female

## LORD HOWE ISLAND STICK INSECT
*Dryococelus australis* ^

In 1918, black rats were introduced to Lord Howe Island (LHI), the home of the once common tree lobster or LHI stick insect. These large, black phasmids were vulnerable to the newly introduced predators and by 1920, the species was thought to be extinct and declared so in 1960. However, 23 kilometres southwest of LHI stands Ball's Pyramid like a knife jutting out of the sea. This steep, volcanic stack has patches of vegetation along its cliffs, and it was rumoured to be home to the last individuals of the LHI stick insect after a team of adventurous climbers saw a dead specimen in 1964. Ball's Pyramid was nearly impossible to access though, and it was not until 2001 that an expedition was dispatched to find the insects. It was then that a population of 24 LHI stick insects was found living on a little paperbark shrub (*Melaleuca howeana*).

Ball's Pyramid was the last outpost for these stick insects.

By 2003, another expedition had secured a breeding pair for the Melbourne Zoo which bred the species successfully in captivity. Today, rodent eradication on LHI and the successful breeding of the LHI stick insect give the species a bright future for reintroduction, but it has yet to be reintroduced to the island.

**Males of this species** are uniquely large like the females. Males, however, have large spines on their hindlegs which they use to fight other males with. These stick insects also sleep together during the day in crevices. At night, they come out to feed and this is when males are thought to fight with one another to access and mate with females. Not much is known about these large phasmids as they were thought to be extinct for nearly 80 years!

Lord Howe Island

^ ***Location:*** *Found only on Lord Howe Island.*

# COMMON STICK INSECTS

## SUBFAMILY PHASMATINAE

**Titan females can be 26cm long, or 36cm long if you include their legs.**

### THE TITAN STICK INSECT

*Acrophylla titan* <

Titan stick insects would more accurately be called branch insects. These phasmids are green as nymphs, which likely helps them blend in with the foliage that they eat. By adulthood, they are too large to blend in with the leaves and will take on a mottled grey-brown colouration that likely helps them blend in with the grey bark or branches of eucalypts (*Eucalyptus* spp.) and paperbarks (*Melaleuca* spp.) that they like to feed on. If they are startled, female titans can flash their large, darkly coloured wings to scare away any potential predator. Male titans are much smaller than females, but their smaller size and more slender body helps them fly to females. The larger body size of females can help them lay more eggs. Entomologist Paul Brock raised one female and over seven months, she laid 2,811 eggs!

> ***Location:*** *East coast of New South Wales and southeast Queensland.*

### TESSELLATED STICK INSECT

*Anchiale austrotessulata* >

Stick insects are famous for their camouflage, but the tessellated stick insect takes this to the next level. It has different colour forms, so it can grow into a brown or green adult. This is thought to depend on what environment they grow up in. They feed on the leaves of eucalypts and wattles, and brown individuals are thought to come from trees with many stick insects present, while green individuals are from sparse populations. So perhaps it's better to resemble the sticks when lots of stick insects are eating all the leaves.

> ***Location:*** *Southeast Queensland and northern New South Wales.*

**These stick insects can turn into green or brown adults! Here, you can see a brown female and a green female mating with the small male.**

**The females** also have very long leaf-shaped appendages at the end of their body, called cerci. These cerci look like another set of arms, potentially making her abdomen appear as a second head.

**The gargantuan stick insect** is the longest stick insect in Australia and the second longest in the world. The record female was 56.5cm long!

**Photograph by:** Alan Henderson – Minibeast Wildlife.

## THE GARGANTUAN STICK INSECT

*Ctenomorpha gargantua* ^

Very few specimens have been found in the wild, shrouding this species in mystery. However, when a bird was seen eating a female in someone's backyard, entomologists from Minibeast Wildlife intervened to recover what they could of this stick insect. The female was unable to be saved, but several eggs were gained from her, and these eggs later hatched into a colony of these long phasmids. Over a year and a half, the small nymphs grew into long adults, showing the long-life of this species. Males are only about one-third the length of females, but they have long wings and can fly.

> ***Location:*** *Tropical North Queensland.*

## CIGAR STICK INSECT

*Cigarrophasma tessellatum* >

True to its name, the cigar stick insect resembles an exotic and expensive looking cigar. Unlike other phasmids, this species is very stocky, but like other phasmids, they can vary in colour from brown to olive green to a black and white lichen colour! Their first line of defence is camouflage and if disturbed, they may drop to the ground, sticking their legs out and pretending to be a fallen stick. This genus was not known to science until 2000 and specimens were only collected in the mid-1990s! What other phasmid wonders await discovery?

> ***Location:*** *Tropical North Queensland.*

**Their second line of defence is to use a startle display. While their wings are too short to fly, they can lift them up to reveal a black and blue alien-like face hidden underneath.**

**By holding their legs out front, stick insects can distort their body shape.**

## GORGON STICK INSECT

*Onchestus gorgus* >

Both males and females of this dark brown, rainforest species have short wings. They also have short spikes on their head resembling a crown and the females have lobes on their legs. When disturbed, they will open their wings and either hold them open or flap them to make a raspy noise. This noise may have other uses, such as attracting a mate or fighting over territory, but behavioural studies must be conducted to determine these uses.

> ***Location:*** *Rainforests of southeast Queensland and northern New South Wales.*

**Photograph:** Ross Coupland.

## THE GOLIATH STICK INSECT

*Eurycnema goliath* ^

The Goliath stick insect is one of the heaviest phasmids in Australia. Adult females have thick abdomens and can be over 20cm long, while males are slender and only up to 16cm long. They both have long, developed hindwings, but the females are too heavy to fly! When their camouflage fails, females will raise their large wings, which are clear with a pink band on one edge. They flap these wings to make a raspy noise, while their spiky hindlegs are opened to show two eyespots near their abdomen. Altogether, this display can frighten away a predator. Goliath nymphs are mottled brown, making them well-camouflaged. After their final moult, these nymphs transform into the bright green, blue, and white adult.

> ***Location:*** *East coast of Australia.*

## RENTZ'S STICK INSECT

*Onchestus rentzi* >

Rentz's stick insect has two spikes on its head. It is common in the tropical rainforests of northern Queensland and paler than its southern sister-species, the gorgon stick insect. It's well hidden in the day but can be more easily found at night when it comes out to feed.

> ***Location:*** *Rainforests of Tropical North Queensland.*

# PALM STICK INSECTS

## SUBFAMILY PLATYCRANINAE

**Females do not need to mate** for their eggs to hatch and several generations of a female only population has been raised in captivity. Their eggs resemble seeds and can take up to 18 months to hatch.

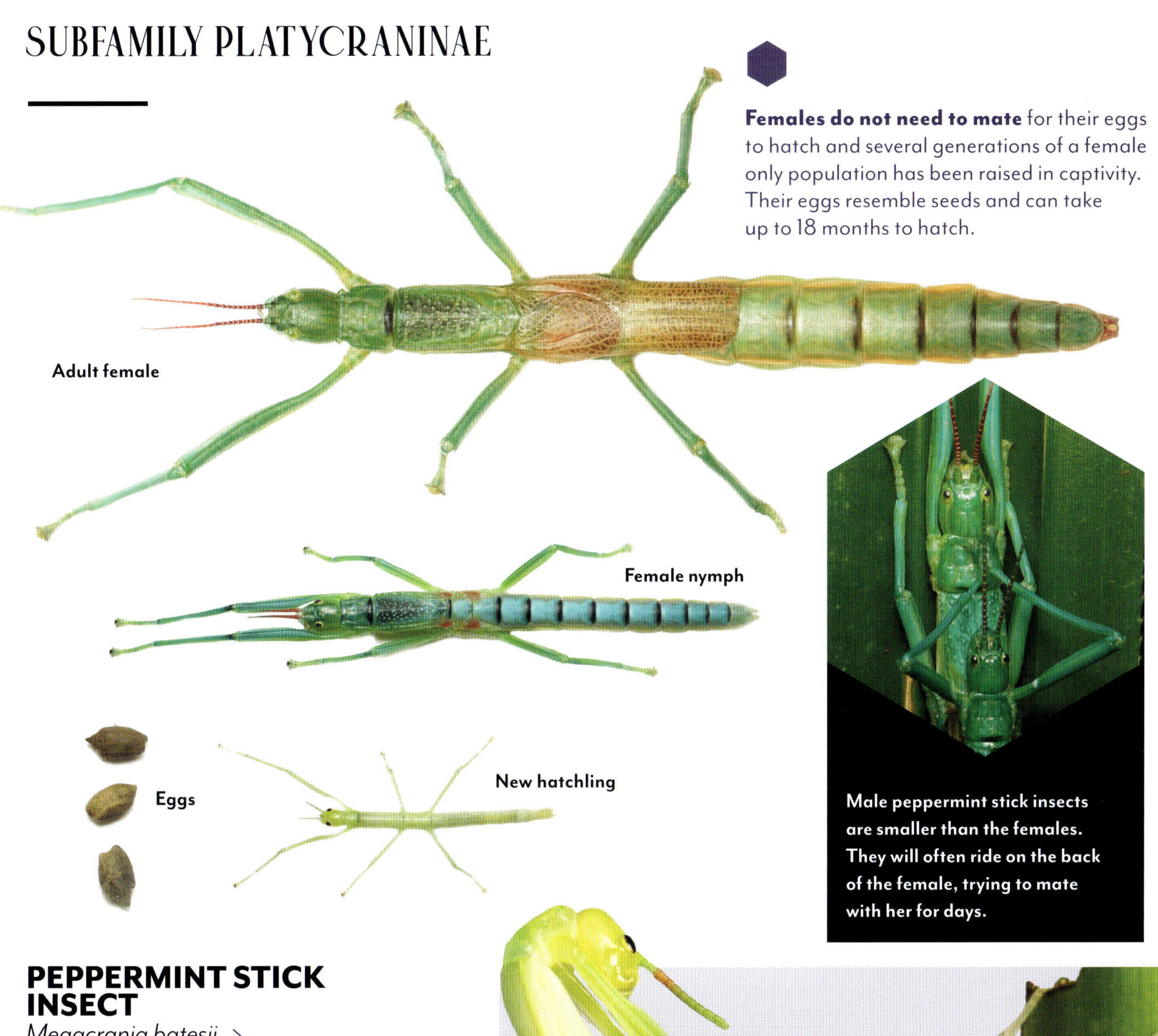


Male peppermint stick insects are smaller than the females. They will often ride on the back of the female, trying to mate with her for days.

### PEPPERMINT STICK INSECT

*Megacrania batesii* >

Peppermint stick insects feed and live inside spiky Pandanus plants. This spiky home helps protect them as they hide between the leaves during the day. They come out at night to feed, loudly chewing their tough host-plant. If a predator finds them though, they quickly slide down the leaves into their safe hiding spot or they can spray their attackers. This spray comes from two openings behind their head and smells like peppermint. The spray can temporarily blind any predators who get too close!

> ***Location:*** *Tropical North Queensland.*

**When the nymphs moult** to grow, they shed not only their exoskeleton, but also the packet of peppermint-scented spray that is kept in a prothoracic gland behind their head.

# GUM STICK INSECTS SUBFAMILY TROPIDODERINAE

## SPINY STICK INSECT
*Extatosoma tiaratum*

The spiny stick insect is one of the easiest and most common species of phasmids to raise. They eat leaves from native plants, but also those from guava (*Psidium guajava*), blackberry, and rose bushes (Family Rosaceae). The females are thicker than the males and have small, reduced wings, while the males are slender with developed wings and long antennae. When a female is ready to lay an egg, she flicks it from the end of her abdomen, letting the egg fall to the ground. Here, it can be picked up by ants that are attracted to the nutritive cap, called a capitulum, on the top of the egg. Ants can carry the eggs back to their nest, where they eat the capitulum and leave the rest of the egg. This can help disperse the eggs and keep them in a moister environment. Up to 19 months later, the egg will hatch into a red and black nymph that resembles an ant. The young nymph will crawl out of the nest and into a host plant, like a eucalypt tree or wattle shrub, where it will feed and spend most of its life.

> ***Location:*** *East coast of Australia.*

Adult male

## HASENPUSCH'S STICK INSECT
*Parapodacanthus hasenpuschorum*

Both males and females of this rainforest species can fly. They are both bright green with large spikes between their head and wings. When females unfold their wings, bright pink colours are visible, and these colours may be used for a startle display. This species also has a defensive spray which is emitted from prothoracic glands located behind their head. The spray smells unpleasant to some, but others have described it as smelling like watermelon bubble gum.

> ***Location:*** *Rainforests in Tropical North Queensland.*

**FACT**

**Rare colour mutations can occur where this species can be yellow or even pink!**

## CHILDREN'S STICK INSECT
*Tropidoderus childrenii*

Children's stick insects are well camouflaged amongst the large eucalypt leaves that they are often found feeding on. If their camouflage fails them, the females can do a startle display by opening and flapping their large wings.Their wings are clear-blue to purple underneath the green coverings. Females are too heavy to fly, but they can use their wings to help them glide. Females can also lay up to 450 eggs and are considered an easy species to raise.

> ***Location:*** *East coast of New South Wales, Southeast Queensland, Victoria and South Australia.*

# LEAF INSECTS FAMILY PHYLLIIDAE

## AUSTRALIAN DANCING LEAF INSECT
*Walaphyllium monteithi*

When they first hatch from their seed-like egg, these leaf insects look like ants! Within a few hours they climb up from the leaf litter to eat leaves and will change from black to green. As they grow, they come to resemble leaves more and more. Some look like a spotty leaf, while others may turn yellow! If their remarkable camouflage fails, these leaves use a defensive spray that smells like cut potatoes. The nymphs and adult females can also make a call by rubbing their antennae together, which may be a distress call. Males and females look very different. Males are slender, with long wings and long antennae to fly to and smell out the females. Females cannot fly, but look more like a leaf.

> ***Location:*** *Tropical North Queensland.*

**Undescribed for decades**

These leaf insects are difficult to find! The first preserved specimens were collected in the 1940s, but they were not found again until 1965 when some high school students found one and turned it in to their teacher. More specimens were collected in the 1970s by Ken Key and Geoff Monteith, two famous Australian entomologists. Despite enough specimens being collected, the species would not be described until 2003 when Paul Brock, a British entomologist and Jack Hasenpusch, a local naturalist worked together.

**FACT**

**They shake or dance as they walk, like a leaf in the wind.**

## THE NANO-LEAF INSECT
*Nanophyllium pygmaeum*

A few collections of small nymphs let scientists know that another, unique leaf insect lived in the Iron Range of northern Queensland, but they could not identify the species until an adult was found. One entomologist, Dave Rentz, found and raised a nymph of the tiny leaf Insect. He fed it and fed it, until one day he looked inside of its cage and wondered if a different insect had crawled inside. Overnight, the small nymph, that resembled a leaf, had moulted into an adult male, that resembled a wasp!

> ***Location:*** *Iron Range / Kutini Payamu National Park, Queensland.*

**Photograph by:** Dave Rentz.

**FACT**

**The adult female of this species was not found until 2022!**

## STORY OF A LOST LOVER

Tiny leaf insects (*Nanophyllium* spp.) are very rare. While males can fly to light traps, females cannot fly, making them nearly impossible to find. In fact, the females of these tiny leaf insects were missing for nearly a century! They were only found when eggs from a leaf insect called *Phyllium asekiense* were sent to the Montreal Insectarium. The males of this leaf insect had also never been found, but these eggs hatched into males and females. The missing males turned out to be tiny leaf insects and the long mystery of the missing counterparts of these two insects was solved. Scientists could not solve this mystery before because the males and females looked like different species with females that resemble leaves and males that look like wasps!

# ABOUT THE AUTHOR

I love insects so much that I moved to Australia! I grew up in Arkansas, USA, where my interest in nature was more of a hobby until I went to university. I thought I wanted to study English and become a writer, but I had to take a science class as part of my degree program. The teacher in this class, Dr. Maureen McClung, inspired me to study biology and entomology and the more that I did, the more I became obsessed. I could not believe that insects are the most diverse group of animals on the planet, yet we know relatively little about their lives!

After finishing university, I came to Australia in 2016 to work on a project with weaver ants and how they impact fruit trees. The insects here were so incredible, that I found myself crying when I had to leave. In 2018, I was able to return and have continued studying and photographing insects here ever since. My research ranges from unravelling the life history of the giant wood moth to studying insect ecology in agriculture to improve pest control. I've also been lucky enough to name the dancing leaf insect (Walaphyllium monteithi) when Royce Cumming discovered it belonged in a unique new genus.

I would not be where I am today without the support of others. When I came to Australia, I was alone, guided by my interest in entomology. Along the way, I met many supportive and brilliant entomologists like Dr. Geoff Monteith. Each time I found an interesting insect, I discovered that Geoff had studied it or that the species was named in his honour! Similarly, Dr. Dave Rentz had described all the interesting katydids, cockroaches, and Cooloola monsters here. When I met each of these entomologists, I nervously introduced myself and soon found supportive mentors in each. The truth of it is: there is much to be known about insects and we are happy to have more people paying attention and contributing. Studying entomology is not about you, but about how incredible the natural world around us is. By studying it, we can know it, appreciate it, and protect it.

This book would also not exist without the support of my partner and fellow entomologist, Andrew Maynard. May this book introduce you to the wonderful world of entomology. You may become an entomologist or general nature nerd. Either way, we need more people caring about the natural world.

Without it, we would be lost.

*Jessa*

# Australia's Incredible Insects

Hardie Grant acknowledges the Traditional Owners of the Country on which we work, the Wurundjeri People of the Kulin Nation and the Gadigal People of the Eora Nation, and recognises their continuing connection to the land, waters and culture. We pay our respects to their Elders past and present.

Hardie Grant Children's Publishing
Wurundjeri Country
Level 11, 36 Wellington Street
Collingwood VIC 3066
Melbourne | Sydney | San Francisco
hardiegrant.com/childrens
www.australiangeographic.com.au

ISBN: 9781761218088

First published 2022
This edition published 2026

A catalogue record for this book is available from the National Library of Australia

**Australian Geographic Original Edition: Editor-in-Chief** Chrissie Goldrick **Author** Jessa Thurman **Creative Director** Mike Ellott **Designer** Mel Tiyce **Editor** Martine Allars **Chief Sub-Editor** Serene Conneeley **Proofreader** Rachelle Mackintosh **Photos** Jessa Thurman, Dr. Chris Burwell, Hongming Kan, Dr. Andrew Maynard, Dr. Dave Rentz, Nick Volpe, Ethan Beaver, François Brassard, Alan Henderson – Minibeast Wildlife, John Lenagan, Stephen Zozaya, John Bromilow, Dianne Clarke, Ross Coupland, Julia Marr, Mitsuhiko Imamori, César Puechmarin, Dr. Peter Samson, Lauren Wade, Alex Wild, Alamy and Shutterstock

**Publisher** Penelope White **Editor** Savannah Hollis **Cover Design** Andy Warren **Internal Design** Hannah Janzen **Production** Sally Davis

Printed in China by LEO Paper Products LTD

The paper this book is printed on is from FSC® certified forests and other controlled sources. FSC® promotes environmentally responsible, socially beneficial and economically viable management of the world's forests.

10 9 8 7 6 5 4 3 2 1